Migration Past, Migration Future

MIGRATION AND REFUGEES
Politics and Policies in the United States and Germany
General Editor: Myron Weiner

Migration Past, Migration Future

Germany and the United States

Edited by
Klaus J. Bade and Myron Weiner

Berghahn Books
Providence • Oxford

First published in 1997 by

Berghahn Books

© 1997 Klaus J. Bade, Myron Weiner

Library of Congress Cataloging-in-Publication Data

```
Migration past, migration future : Germany and the United States /
  edited by Klaus J. Bade and Myron Wiener.
      p.   cm. -- (Migration and refugees ; v. 1)
  Includes bibliographical references and index.
  ISBN 1-57181-125-7 (alk. paper)
  1. United States--Emigration and immigration--Government policy.
2. Immigrants--United States.  3. Refugees--United States.
4. Germany--Emigration and immigration--Government policy.
5. Immigrants--Germany.  6. Refugees--Germany.   I. Bade, Klaus J.
II. Weiner, Myron.  III. Series.
  JV6483.M54  1997 vol. 1
  325.43--dc21                                         97-7505
                                                          CIP
```

British Library Cataloguing in Publication Data

A catalogue record for this book is available from the British Library.

Printed in the United States on acid-free paper.

Contents

Introduction

Klaus J. Bade and *Myron Weiner*

Among the advanced industrial countries the United States and Germany have the largest number of immigrants. In 1993 the United States had 23 million foreign-born residents, or 8.9 percent of the population. The comparable figures for Germany (in 1994) were 6.8 million foreigners (8.6 percent of the population) and 3 million ethnic German immigrants. Since 1988 the migration into Germany of asylum seekers, ethnic Germans from Eastern Europe and the former Soviet Union, new labor migrants, and family members of already established labor migrants has averaged more than 500,000 per year. During this same period the annual migration flows to the United States ranged from 750,000 to 1 million; another 2.6 million illegal migrants who had entered earlier were granted immigrant status, and an estimated 300,000 illegal migrants were entering and staying in the United States each year. In both countries migration issues loom large on the political agenda, partly because it is widely believed that migrants impose fiscal costs on local and national budgets, partly because of concerns over the impact of migration on the local labor market, and partly because the ethnic, racial, or religious composition of the migrants raises issues of acculturation. In both countries there are controversies over whom to admit, how many, and what benefits immigrants should receive. Political leaders have spoken out against migration, and there have been clashes between immigrants and the local population in Los Angeles, New York, and Miami and violent attacks against migrants in the German towns of Hoyerswerda, Mölln, Rostock, and Solingen.

This is the first of a series of five volumes dealing with the refugee and migration issues facing the United States and Germany sponsored by the American Academy of Arts and Sciences with financial support from the German-American Academic Council Foundation. Three working groups were convened by the Academy, each composed of participants from both countries and including lawyers, political scientists, demographers, historians, political philosophers, sociologists, economists, and government officials. A joint German-American steering committee took responsibility for structuring the initial agendas and determining the membership of the working groups. One working group addressed policies toward countries of origin; a second examined admission policies, political asylum, and the crisis of controls; and a third focused on the absorption of migrants. In addition to the five volumes of research papers written by the participants, the project has published a report, "German and American Migration and Refugee Policies: Recommendations of the Joint German-American Project of the American Academy of Arts and Sciences," prepared by the three working groups.

Three of the four papers in this volume (Reed Ueda's paper was added later) were prepared to provide the participants in the project with an understanding of the historical context within which both countries address the issues posed by a large immigrant population and to furnish demographic projections of what the two countries might look like over the next quarter of a century given the present and anticipated future migrant population.

Before reviewing the major themes of this volume it is of interest to note that the migration histories of the two countries have been closely linked. According to the first U.S. census in 1790, about a twelfth of the U.S. population was of German descent. About 90 percent of the Germans who emigrated in the nineteenth century went to the United States and nearly one-sixth of all immigrants who came to the United States between 1820 and 1945 were from Germany, making Germany the largest single source of immigrants during this period. Beyond the numbers, German immigrants had a considerable impact on the creation of industrial, financial, and commercial establishments in the United States. Germans built Bausch and Lomb, Hershey, Heinz, Berlitz, Anheuser-Busch, Miller, Coors, Pabst, Schlitz, Steinway pianos, and Wurlitzer organs. German immigrants and ethnic Germans also influenced the structure of the U.S. university system, medical education, and even the organization of the military (Generals Pershing and Eisenhower were of German descent). With the rise of the Nazi regime many German and German-speaking intellectuals, mostly but not entirely Jewish, fled to the United States. Their influence on American intellectual life—on science, mathematics, literature, music, philosophy, architecture, linguistics, art history, and the social sciences—is incalculable.

It is not, however, the influence of German immigrants on the United States that is the subject of this book but rather the impact that migration has had and is having on the two societies. Migration assumed an important new role in both countries after the Second World War, and for similar reasons. A labor shortage during the Second World War led the United States to recruit workers from Mexico to meet the growing demand for agricultural laborers. The guest-worker program continued after the war and was not terminated until 1964, by which time a chain migration was in place that led to a continuous influx of legal and illegal migrants. By 1994 Mexican Americans constituted the largest single immigrant group in the country: 6.3 million Mexican-born residents. A second development in U.S. migration policy was the ending of the long-standing racial restrictions on migration. The transformation of American attitudes and policies during the civil rights movement facilitated the passage of the 1965 immigration act that opened the door to migrants from Asia. Migrants from Asia—China, Korea, India, and Southeast Asia—soon outnumbered the legal flows from Europe and even from Latin America. A third development was the adoption of refugee policies that enabled individuals from Communist countries to come to the United States: from Cuba, Eastern Europe, the Soviet Union, Cambodia, Laos, and Vietnam.

To a certain extent similar factors were at work in Germany, where the employment of foreign workers had a tradition dating back to the decades before the First World War. During the Second World War Germany met its labor shortages by employing forced foreign laborers, especially from German-occupied Eastern Europe. After the war these workers were returned home, while the redrawing of the borders in Central Europe, flight, and expulsion led to a massive movement of an estimated 12 million Germans into Germany from East Central and Eastern Europe. In the mid-1950s, however, Germany again began to recruit foreign workers, the so-called guest workers, this time mainly from Italy, Greece, Spain, Portugal, Yugoslavia, and Turkey, to meet the labor shortages of its high-growth economy. The flow of guest workers was accelerated when the German Democratic Republic sealed its borders with the construction of the Berlin Wall in 1961. The guest-worker program was terminated in 1973, but millions of workers chose to remain in Germany, where they were joined by their families. By 1979, therefore, Germany had more immigrants than in 1973, and through family unification and marriages (what has been characterized as "reproductive migration") the flow continues. Klaus J. Bade writes that "more than in any other Western industrial state during the second half of this century, the population, economy, and society in West Germany have been characterized by mass migration movements."

West Germany also accepted refugees from Communist countries. There were flows across the borders when Soviet forces crushed the political uprisings in Hungary and Czechoslovakia, and a limited but continuous flow of citizens occurred from the German Democratic Republic to West Germany. When the government of Hungary opened its borders to Austria in July and August 1989, hundreds of thousands of East Germans exited into West Germany. Forced to choose between closing its borders to the east or opening them to the west, the German Democratic Republic opened its western borders. The result was a massive migration westward followed by the fall of the GDR and the absorption of East Germany by the Federal Republic of Germany.

In somewhat different ways ethnic considerations played a role in both the U.S. and German postwar migration and refugee policies. Under German law ethnic Germans from the eastern part of the European continent whose ancestors had emigrated generations and even centuries earlier had the legal right to return and reclaim their citizenship on the assumption that they had been suffering from repression caused by the war. For several decades only a limited number of ethnic Germans in

Eastern Europe and the Soviet Union could avail themselves of the opportunity, but much larger numbers could do so by the late 1980s. In the 1990s they were coming at the rate of more than 200,000 per year. In the United States, though ethnic criteria were officially eliminated from immigration law, ethnic considerations played a role in the decision to classify Jews from the Soviet Union as refugees (Germany adopted this same position) and to continue to treat all Cubans as refugees. Ethnic considerations also entered into a congressional decision to introduce a "diversity" category into migration law that enabled more citizens from Ireland to migrate to the United States.

There is now a considerable demographic convergence in the two countries with respect to their immigrant populations. Both countries have new immigrant populations that are different from those that earlier settled in the two countries. In the nineteenth and early part of the twentieth century migrants to the United States were predominantly from Europe, and to Germany (especially Prussia) the foreign workers were largely Poles from the Russian and Austrian parts of Poland and Italians. The new migrants to the United States come from Asia and Latin America, and the German guest workers, forming the great bulk of the foreign population, mainly came from southeastern Europe and Turkey. In both countries there are also large numbers of migrants who have ethnic ties with the local population: ethnic Germans from Eastern Europe and the former Soviet Union in Germany, and in the United States Mexicans and Jews from the former Soviet Union. Both countries admitted substantial numbers of refugees from Communist countries, and to a limited extent both have been admitting refugees from the so-called third world. And both countries now have a substantial working-class immigrant community from low-income emigration countries. The percentage of immigrants as a proportion of the population, as we have already indicated, is remarkably similar.

The two countries have responded to these demographic changes quite differently, however, influenced by their divergent histories and conceptions of citizenship and nationality. Germany has historically been mainly a country of emigration, although in the early modern history of Germany there were several streams of immigrants, including refugees from religious persecution. Throughout the nineteenth century emigration from Germany provided an outlet for a growing population that was displaced as the country made the transition from an agricultural to an industrial society, accompanied by a disproportionate growth of population and the economy. Emigration was regarded by many Germans as a sociopolitical necessity, a way of reducing the dangers of a social revolution by providing an outlet for the underemployed. At the same time it was hoped that the migrants would retain their "Germanness." In 1913 a citizenship law based on the jus sanguinis principle was passed that enabled Germans living abroad to maintain and inherit German citizenship. Germany's efforts to protect and maintain ties with its emigrants has its parallels in the present efforts of the governments of Turkey and Mexico to protect and maintain ties with their migrants to Germany and the United States.

While Germans were emigrating to the West, Poles were migrating into Germany, where they were recruited especially by Prussian employers. Although their labor was welcomed, the Prussian state feared "polonization" and took measures to ensure that Polish workers from abroad would not be incorporated as citizens. Even as the citizenship law of 1913 sought to extend the rights to citizenship of ethnic Germans living abroad, it limited the acquisition of German citizenship by foreigners. The ethnic conception of the nation-state and the separation of territory from citizenship was then and continues to be at the core of the idea of German nationality. Thus ethnic Germans from the East can continue to return to Germany to reclaim their citizenship, while the native-born children of foreigners have no automatic entitlement to citizenship. There are foreigners with German passports, that is, ethnic Germans, and Germans with foreign passports, that is, the second- or even third-generation descendants of former guest workers. Indeed, under a new "residence permit requirement" order promulgated in January 1997, the German-born children of former guest workers who are not from European Union countries must apply for separate visas.

In the United States, writes Reed Ueda, citizenship and nationality were equivalent. "All citizens were members of the nation and all members of the nation were equal citizens," although, one should note, blacks and Native Americans were for much of U.S. history excluded from this universal benefit.

The United States developed a civic culture that emphasized the free expression of ideas, the rights of groups to organize for political action, and the separation of church and state and drew a clear distinction between the public and the private realm. "Americanism" in a cultural and political sense was inculcated in the schools, but individuals and the groups with which they identified were free to express their own ethnic identities, create their own religious institutions, publish newspapers in their own languages, and use politics to pursue their own interests. Even apart from blacks and Native Americans, in practice the system of assimilative ethnic pluralism had many flaws—Asians had been excluded from citizenship and many Japanese Americans were interned during the Second World War—but overall the effect was a vibrancy in U.S. society and an economy opened to millions of newcomers.

How the system of assimilative pluralism shaped the lives of immigrants has been the subject of extensive research. In his essay Reed Ueda provides an informative case study of how German immigrants to the United States—seven million came from 1820 to 1990—contributed to U.S. agriculture, industry, artisanship, education, cuisine, and religion and also of how their distinctive communal identity was eventually eroded in large part as a consequence of the two world wars.

The controversies over migration that presently engulf U.S. politics have as much to do with the future as with the present. Will the Asian and Latin American immigrants in the United States become as integrated into U.S. culture and civic life as previous generations of immigrants? Will low-skilled migrants from the Caribbean and Mexico become socially mobile and acculturated or will they become part of an underclass, contributing to crime, drug addiction, and teenage pregnancies? Will highly educated immigrants significantly contribute to scientific creativity, economic productivity, and international competitiveness, but will they also take jobs away from the native population? Will immigrants impose financial burdens on the welfare state and on the educational system, or in the course of their lifetimes will they financially contribute more than they take out?

The study by Frank Bean, Robert Cushing, and Charles Haynes of the University of Texas at Austin starts with the central question: Are recent concerns about levels of immigration in the United States a reflection more of anxieties about changes in the size of racial/ethnic groups or of worries about economic competition and job opportunities? They report that the United States is being transformed from a society with a white majority and small black and smaller Native American minority into a very diverse multiethnic, multiracial society. This transformation is the result of three factors: (1) the changing ethnic and racial composition of legal and illegal migration to the United States since 1965; (2) a migration flow equal to the highest in any period of U.S. history; and (3) a significantly higher number of births among immigrants than among the native born. One consequence is the increasing pressure on urban school enrollments. In New York City, for example, four in every ten births are to immigrants. In 1990 29 percent of the women in the city were foreign-born, but they had 43 percent of the children. A second consequence is that an increasing proportion of the population is Hispanic, Asian, or black, projected to increase from 24.8 percent of the total population in 1990 to 37.5 percent in 2020, with most of the increase among Asians and Hispanics. A third consequence is that more than one-third of the U.S. population growth (which increased by 2.3 million in 1996) can be attributed to annual immigration. The proportion is substantially higher if one includes births to immigrant families.

Critics of immigration are concerned that the result will be interracial and interethnic conflict, growing competition for jobs as population increases faster than the rate of labor force growth, and increased costs for the welfare and education systems. In addressing these issues Bean, Cushing, and Haynes report a high and growing intermarriage rate between the Asian and Latin American immigrant population and the native white population. As the boundaries between groups become blurred, projections of the country's racial and ethnic composition become uncertain. Moreover, as acculturation by immigrants takes place, the central question is, acculturation to what? Some immigrants will follow the well-trodden path of social mobility, while others may become acculturated to the economically least successful and most alienated social classes. As to the impact of immigrants on the labor market (both on wages and employment of native workers) and on fiscal matters (the balance of taxes paid to federal, state, and local government and what immigrants and their children receive in turn) they conclude that the effects are not particularly large, whether positive or negative, but that a slow growth in the labor force and wage stagnation do affect public attitudes toward immigration and immigrants. They also point to the failure of the government to control undocumented immigration, the inclusion of legal immigrants in affirmative action policies, and the heavy burden that immigration imposes on many local government budgets as factors affecting public attitudes toward migration. Many Americans are also concerned that the emphasis on multiculturalism and bilingualism does not encourage new immigrants to take pride in U.S. history and civic values or even to speak English.

Some of the widely held concerns stem from a lack of understanding of the historical experiences with migrants earlier in this century. Prior to the First World War many immigrant families also received public assistance and were dependent on public hospitals for their medical care. Their children were a heavy financial burden on the school systems of Chicago, New York, and other major cities, and in the 1870s and 1880s several state governments filed suit against the central government seeking to recover some of the immigrant-related costs. The new arrivals also lived in ethnic enclaves where they continued to speak their mother tongues. Recent studies show that mobility rates for the second generation were not particularly high and it often took three or four generations before the descendants of immigrants reached educational and economic parity with natives. The United States is, of course, now very different from what it was earlier in the century. There are fewer opportunities for advancement by unskilled workers; public schools have deteriorated and are less likely to provide the children of uneducated migrants (and uneducated Americans) with the kind of education that would furnish them with the skills they need for job mobility; and there are legitimate concerns that in some parts of the country where there are high concentrations of immigrants bilingual education may slow English language acquisition. For these and other reasons educational reform is high on the political agenda.

The demographic study of German migration by Rainer Münz and Ralf Ulrich disaggregates the different flows into postwar Germany: ethnic Germans *(Aussiedler)* from Eastern Europe and the former Soviet Union; citizens of the GDR *(übersiedler)*

moving to the FRG; the return to Germany of some of its overseas migrants; foreign workers recruited mainly from Italy,
Greece, Spain, Yugoslavia and Turkey, and the de facto settlement of large numbers of guest workers after recruitment was
halted in 1973; and since 1988 a substantial rise in the number
of asylum seekers and refugees from former Yugoslavia and the
so-called third world. As a result of the rise in public opposition
to migration and the violent attacks against foreigners, the German government adopted measures to make entry more difficult
by restricting asylum seekers. In 1994, write Münz and Ulrich,
half of all foreigners had been in Germany for over ten years, one
in four for more than twenty, and of the 7 million foreign nationals 1.2 million were born in Germany but did not have German
citizenship. In 1994 13 percent of all children born in Germany
were born to foreigners and, given current citizenship law, automatically became foreigners. Since most of the foreigners live in
large cities, the percentage of foreigners in some cities is considerably higher than the national average: well over 20 percent in
Frankfurt, Stuttgart, and Munich. "It is," they write, "a characteristic of Germany as a self-declared nonimmigration country
that the naturalization of foreign immigrants and their children
is still the exception, not the rule."

What will be the ethnic composition of Germany in the early
part of the twenty-first century? Münz and Ulrich suggest three
alternative scenarios, taking into account the population growth
rates of both the German and foreign populations as well as
migration and naturalization rates. For each scenario they
derive estimates as to the future growth of the foreign population in Germany to the year 2030. Their striking finding is that
"even if there were a quasi-standstill in the immigration of foreigners, their share among total population would still almost
double within the next thirty-four years," in part because of the
growing excess of deaths over births among native Germans.
The foreign minority will increase from an estimated 7 million
in 1995 to 11.9 million in 2015 to 14.2 million in 2030. (In the
absence of the contribution of migrants to population growth,
Germany's population would decline. Indeed, it is estimated
that immigration accounts for three-quarters of the European
Union's annual population growth of 1.1 million.) In several of
West Germany's largest cities the foreign population will range

from 30 to 45 percent with comparable proportions or more in the schools. Without a reconceptualization of Germany from an ethnonational society in which citizenship is based on ethnic identity to a society in which membership in the political system is acquired by birth and choice, Germany will not be able to integrate its immigrant population and their children. It is in danger of becoming a society deeply divided between those who have full membership and those who are excluded.

In both countries the integration of immigrants is also likely to be influenced by developments within the source countries. A deterioration of the economy or political system of Mexico, Central America, or the countries of the Caribbean could precipitate a flow that could adversely affect the migrants from these countries already in the United States. Similarly, if Islamic fundamentalism should increase or clashes with Kurdish insurgents intensify within Turkey, there could be spillover effects within Germany; the incorporation of Poland into the European Union could also generate a new substantial movement of workers from Poland. In both countries—and indeed in any country that receives significant numbers of migrants from other cultures—tensions and even conflicts between migrants and sections of the local population are likely. It is at these moments that politicians respond. The response can be a focus on law and order, tightening of borders, and restrictions on the migrant population, or it can be an effort to find a common ground among individuals from different cultures who must live and work together. How the two countries deal with these conflicts has implications for their societies and polities that go well beyond the question of how they deal with their migrant populations.

We are grateful to the German-American Academic Council Foundation for its financial support for the project and to its director, Dr. Joseph Rembser; the Gottlieb Daimler- and Karl Benz-Foundation for its support for a meeting of the participants in Ladenburg, Germany; our editor Sarah St. Onge; Lois Malone, administrative assistant to Myron Weiner; and Corinne Schelling of the American Academy of Arts and Sciences, who has had principal responsibility for the management of the project since its inception.

Chapter 1

From Emigration to Immigration

The German Experience in the Nineteenth and Twentieth Centuries

Klaus J. Bade

New Challenges and Forgotten Experiences

United Germany has become more ethnically diverse and, to a certain extent, more multicultural, with a growing minority of immigrants and temporary migrants living within its borders. There are labor migrants from Southern and Eastern Europe with restricted work permits, immigrants coming out of the former "guest-worker" population, and ethnic Germans from Eastern Europe as well as various groups of asylum seekers and other refugees (Schmalz-Jacobsen and Hansen 1995; Heckmann 1992).

Facing migration problems is a new and threatening experience for many Germans. Contemporary public debate has largely chosen to ignore the fact that throughout German history the movement of people across borders and the consequent clash of cultures has not been the exception but the norm. It has also been forgotten that many native inhabitants are descendants of foreigners who immigrated to Germany and that millions of German emigrants were strangers in foreign countries, just as many foreigners today are strangers in the united Germany.

Notes for this chapter can be found on page 32.

Another historical reminder that should be called back into public consciousness is the numerous "Little Germanies" in the transatlantic New World of the nineteenth century that have existed for two or three generations, much as the "Little Istanbuls" and other ethnic communities exist in German cities today. If Berlin is called today's largest Turkish city outside of Turkey, it should be recalled that in the United States in the nineteenth century many more or less German towns and city neighborhoods could be found throughout the country, not just in the predominantly German Midwest.

In the past, Germans abroad and foreigners in Germany have experienced all imaginable forms of cross-border migrations: emigration, immigration, and transit movements; the labor migration of Germans across German borders and the influx of foreign labor into Germany; flight and forced migration of Germans into foreign countries, of foreigners into Germany, and of Germans as victims and offenders within and outside German national borders. In addition to the movement of people across borders, German history has also seen the movement of borders across people. Finally, in recent German history, there have been enormous domestic migrations, often over large distances, which have made even former inlanders become strangers in Germany itself. This was true, for example, for the long-distance migrations of the "Ruhr Poles" and the "Ruhr Masures" from Eastern Prussia to the coal and steel industries of the Prussian West as well as for the migration of refugees and expellees from the former German east after World War II (Bade 1992, 1994b).

As this discussion shows, encounters of the majority with minorities and of native inhabitants with foreigners have been frequent and common in German history. It should be possible, therefore, to handle the consequent issues and problems in a pragmatic, even calm manner. Some of these issues, however, carry the weight of tragedy. This is all the more true as German history has seen not only the migration of people across borders and of borders across people but also the exclusion of minorities, such as ethnic Poles, Jews, Sinti, and Rom within German borders. In this context belongs a development from the nationalistic and romantically *(völkisch-romantisch)* inspired dissociation of the "other" *(Fremde)* in the early nineteenth century, the ethnonationalistic agitation against "alienness" *(Fremdartigkeit)* in the late nineteenth and early twentieth centuries, and the systematic racist destruction of "culturally alien stock" *(Artfremde)* in Nazi Germany and German-occupied Europe. The horrible end of this path casts its long-lasting shadow of mass crimes committed against ethnic, cultural, religious, and other minorities (Hoffmann 1994).

A necessary condition for acquiring the capacity to tolerate the foreign is a positive relationship to one's own, since feelings of positive collective social identity (we-ness) offer a sense of security. Therefore, in Germany, the historical relationship to one's own, scarred by the darkest chapter of German history, is in itself a burden. This is particularly relevant when criteria, quota, and other basic regulations of immigrant policies are debated.

The memory of the fact that in Nazi Germany and in German-occupied Europe millions of Jews and other victims were deprived of their rights, persecuted, and murdered complicates the discussion of minority issues, of quota regulations, and of the inevitably resulting problems of inclusion and exclusion. The shadows of the past continue to darken the present when public discussion compares decision-making processes regarding potential immigrants' applications to the "selection" at the ramps of Nazi concentration camps. Be that as it may, Germany cannot avoid creating legislative and political structures to cope with the problems of immigration, integration, and minorities. This former country of emigration, an unwilling immigration country today, has to deal more and more with problems that in former times were more often caused by Germans abroad.

From Transatlantic Emigration to Continental Immigration

Emigration has a long historical tradition for Germans. Indeed, it has not ceased even today, although it is fading and becoming largely irrelevant, especially when compared with the much more frequent immigration from other regions into German territory. An early example of emigration from German-speaking regions includes the migration from the Rhine and Mosel areas to the Hungarian Kingdom in the mid-twelfth century. These migrants, called *Siebenbürger Sachsen* in Hungary (Transylvania), were followed in the eighteenth century by other groups of settlers, called *Banater* and *Sathmarer Schwaben* in their new world in Southeast Europe.

There were also German settlements in other central and southeastern European regions. For a long time, they were accorded special economic, legal, and cultural privileges, the settlements in Wolhynia, for example, as well as those on the Crimean peninsula and in the Caucasus, all in multiethnic czarist Russia. Another significant settlement in Russia was at the Volga, where the Autonomous Soviet Republic of the Volga Germans was founded in 1924. In 1941, in response to Hitler's attack on the Soviet Union, Stalin ordered the destruction of this republic. The German settlers were deported to the eastern border of the Soviet Empire. Since the fall of the Iron Curtain, millions of ethnic Germans from the East *(Aussiedler)* and their descendants are, as they themselves and official German policies put it, returning to their ancestors' homeland in great numbers. This mass "re"-migration, which began in the 1950s, changed to a continental mass immigration in the late 1980s (Dralle 1991; Brandes 1992, 85–134).

It was not until the 1830s that the flow of continental emigration from Germany to the East was surpassed by the transatlantic mass emigration to the West, with 90 percent of the latter directed to the United States. Other, less important destinations of transatlantic emigration from Germany were Canada, Brazil, Argentina, and Australia.

Estimates of the number of Germans who may have immigrated during the colonial period range from about 65,000 to about 100,000. At the time of the American Revolution, approximately 225,000 German-Americans made up about 8 to 9 percent of the total population of the colonies and, according to the first U.S. census in 1790, about a twelfth of the U.S. population was then of German descent (Helbich, Kamphoefner, and Sommer 1988, 11; Moltmann 1982, 9).

The primarily religiously oriented group migrations leading to community settlements were without doubt of significance in the German emigration to North America during the colonial era. Overinterpretation of religious motives should, however, be avoided: "The motives for emigration were always complex, economic and social problems were always important, and often decisive" (Helbich, Kamphoefner, and Sommer 1988, 29). In fact, growing numbers of emigrants without any apparent religious motivation or even group membership had already found their way to the New World in the eighteenth century. That was above all true of those for whom the redemptioner system, which can be traced from 1728 through the American Revolution and into the 1820s, opened the way across the Atlantic. According to reliable estimates, one-half to two-thirds of the German immigrants to British North America were redemptioners. There were also even earlier cases of mass migration leading thousands of Germans to North America in the eighteenth century (1709, 1749 to 1752, 1757, 1759, 1782). Apart from the rapid increase in the number of emigrants to about 20,000 in 1816 to 1817, as a result of a poor harvest and a famine, numbers remained relatively low until the mid-1830s (Moltmann 1979; Focke 1976, 63–100). It was not until the first half of the nineteenth century that this level was to any great extent exceeded (Helbich, Kamphoefner, and Sommer 1988, 32; Moltmann 1982, 10; 1986, 105–22; cf. von Hippel 1984, 35ff., 41, 132; Fenske 1980, 332–47).

From 1816 to 1914, about 5.5 million Germans emigrated to the United States, followed, since 1914, by another 1.5 million. From 1820 to 1860, the German-born population formed the second-largest group of immigrants to the United States (30 percent), after the Irish, and from 1861 to 1890 Germans represented the largest immigrant group. Overall, since 1820 Germans have accounted for about 15 percent of European immigration, making them the largest group of European immigrants. According to a survey conducted in 1979, Germany is the country in which the greatest number of Americans believe they have family roots: about 26 percent of the Americans polled believed they could trace at least some of their ancestors back to Germany. Today, transatlantic nostalgia characterizes the expanding business of the "routes to the roots" on both sides of the Atlantic. Recently, considerable sums of private and public money have been invested in this business on the German side.

Transatlantic emigration from nineteenth-century Germany was primarily a socioeconomic mass movement composed of small groups, families, and later, to an increasing extent, of individual migrants. This pattern differed from previous transatlantic emigration, which was dominated by groups leaving for religious reasons or hoping to build utopian, early socialist, or communist communities. The traces of these groups, however, had already faded in the first half of the nineteenth century, with the rising and mass movement that characterized transatlantic emigration in the second half of the century. During this period, and particularly in the last third of the nineteenth century, conditions of transatlantic migration changed: travel on steamships became more bearable, more frequent, and less expensive. At the same time, the extension of railway networks made the trip to the port of exit and the continuation of the journey from seaports within the country of immigration easier and faster. Furthermore, increasing transatlantic communication as well as migration traditions formed by the mass movement were supporting factors in many emigration areas. Letters from emigrants, prepaid tickets, and chain migrations served to ease decisions to emigrate.

The German dream of America encompassed a broad variety of hopes, expectations, and counterimages of the New World. The primary motives for the transatlantic mass emigration from nineteenth-century Germany remained, however, economic and social, the most important being the disproportion between population growth and labor opportunities. The cause of this disproportion was the crucial transition from an agrarian to an industrial society. Using today's terminology, it can be said that most German emigrants during the nineteenth century were "economic refugees" *(Wirtschaftsflüchtlinge)* in the true sense of the phrase.

After the sharp rise in emigration figures between the mid-1830s and the mid-1840s, transatlantic emigration can be characterized as a "proletarian mass migration" (Ferenczi 1929, 81ff.) As a mass movement, it must be viewed against a background of population growth, profound changes in social institutions, and rapid economic transformation. The millionfold emigration from nineteenth-century Germany, which had the effect of exporting social problems, served to relieve widespread social tensions in the home country (Fenske 1973, 221–36; Hansen 1976, 8–61; Kuckhoff 1976, 102–45).

This became particularly evident during the first emigration wave (1846 to 1857), initiated by Germany's last preindustrial crisis of the disastrous *type ancien* (Labrousse 1943) in 1846 to 1847, which struck both agriculture and the crafts (Labrousse 1932, 1943; cf. Abel 1974, 302–96). This crisis pushed the emigration curve above the level of the revolutionary period to 176,402 in 1852. From there, figures rose sharply to the 1854 peak of 239,246, when emigration increasingly took on the nature of a mass flight to the New World. The mass movement lowered the threshold of individual decision making and developed its own momentum ("emigration fever"). Between the last crisis of the type ancien and the start of the "first world economic crisis" (Rosenberg 1974) in 1857 to 1859, nearly 1.3 million Germans emigrated overseas, more than half a million of them moving between 1854 and 1857 alone (Rosenberg 1974). The defeat of the 1848/49 revolution and the subsequent period of political reaction reinforced the tendency to emigrate, but with the exception of the small group of Forty-Eighters, emigration for purely political reasons did not increase (Zucker 1950; Wittke 1952; Dobert 1958; Kamphoefner 1980, 89–102).

The outbreak of the American Civil War in 1861 led to a short-term congestion of the emigration stream, but by 1864, before the end of the war, the second emigration wave had begun to swell. During the economic recession from 1873 to 1879, which affected the German and the U.S. economies equally, emigration figures again fell sharply. Immediately after the end of the recession, however, the third and largest emigration wave of the nineteenth century started abruptly, in 1880. It brought almost 1.8 million emigrants, until the U.S. economic crisis in 1893 effectively ended this last emigration wave from nineteenth-century Germany.

All in all, the exodus to America was a flight from the penurious social circumstances of the Old World. Though sustained by dreams of liberty, above all it was spurred by the hope for better economic and social living conditions in the New World. Many emigrants crossed the Atlantic hoping to regain their lost economic status, to realize dreams that the Old World could not fulfill, or even to export overseas a basis of economic livelihood that was threatened at home. This was true for many farm laborers and sons of farmers not in line to inherit land who hoped to become independent farmers in the United States. In many cases, particularly in the last third of the nineteenth century, these emigrants ended up as factory workers. This often represented a painful step into modern economy and society, and in many cases the result of emigration was precisely what the newcomers had hoped to avoid by leaving their home countries. Expectations for new lives did not always match the realities of the New World.

The greatest mass movement crossed the Atlantic during the five decades from 1846 to 1893, with more than 100,000 emigrants in the 1850s and more than 200,000 per year in the 1880s. Between 1880 and 1893 there were still approximately 1.8 million emigrants heading overseas. After that, the secular mass emigration from nineteenth-century Germany declined as demographic pressure was more and more absorbed at home by the increasing employment opportunities of the industrial labor market. The boom period that started in the mid-1890s, in spite of two recessions, lasted until the eve of World War I, replacing transatlantic emigration to a certain degree with the increasing streams of internal migration from rural to urban-industrial areas.

A new gigantic wave of emigration from Germany was expected to start after World War I, particularly after the treaty of Versailles. However, German emigration in 1919 and 1920 was of no significance. After the gradual removal of the barriers to emigration that had been erected because of the war, migration increased considerably, but it was only in 1923 that it reached a level comparable to the emigration waves of the nineteenth century. During the period of industrial stabilization in the mid-1920s emigration slowly declined, and at the beginning of the world economic crisis—the Great Depression—it stopped abruptly, only to resume after 1933, with the flight of hundreds of thousands from political and racist persecution in Nazi Germany.

This new movement can by no means be compared to the German transatlantic emigration during the preceding one hundred years (Bade 1986, 259–99; Doerries 1987, 115–34). Nazi barbarity accounted for the exceptional mass flight from German-speaking regions. Even today the extent of this flight can only be estimated, because considerable numbers of emigrants crossed borders illegally or traveled in disguise, leaving no traces in the emigration statistics. In any case, the total number of refugees from German-speaking countries to other European countries or overseas from 1933 to 1945 is estimated to be well over half a million; the number of emigrants of Jewish origin alone reached more than 500,000.

Emigration from German-speaking countries during the Nazi period can be traced to nearly eighty countries of destination all over the world. States bordering Germany were mainly transit countries until the German war machine broke through their borders. The United States was the last and most important country of refuge, absorbing about 48 percent of the emigrants. From 1933 to 1941, the year in which the USA entered World War II, a total of 104,098 Germans and Austrians, of which more than 80 percent were Jews, emigrated to the United States. Roughly half of these, however, did not arrive until 1938 to 1941, because most fled first to surrounding European countries and then continued their flight from there to the States as the threat of German expansion grew during the war. For many, especially for the Jewish emigrants, the flight into exile and emigration was a salvation from the imminent threat to their lives (Röder and Strauss, 1980–83; Benz 1991).

After World War II a gigantic mass emigration from Germany, overpopulated with refugees and economically ruined, was once again anticipated. Emigration during the immediate postwar years, however, was only possible for a very limited number of people and for special reasons. Thereafter, the transatlantic movement, although it was permitted once again, did not reach the proportions that initially had been expected. In 1948 approximately 27,400 emigrants left Germany. In 1952 the rate reached the postwar peak, with approximately 90,000 emigrants, and in 1956 82,000 Germans headed overseas. After that, the numbers declined consistently, and in 1960, the first year of full employment, about 47,700 people emigrated from Germany. Among the countries of destination, the United States was still the most popular, followed by Canada, Australia, and Brazil.

Expellees and refugees made up a high contingent of the emigration from postwar Germany: in 1956 they represented 17.5 percent of the overall residential population of West Germany, yet they made up 37 percent of overseas migrants for that year. As their integration into the Federal Republic progressed, they accounted for a decreasing fraction of the total overseas emigration (Bethlehem 1982, 205–9).

As a result of the increasing development of international labor markets, emigration became a nineteenth century concept for most of the Germans who went abroad in the 1960s. Today only a small percentage of the Germans leaving the country annually are emigrants in the nineteenth-century sense of leaving without any intention of permanent return. The traditional understanding of emigration as a permanent departure from one's country has been replaced by modern patterns of seeking education and training in other countries, working for German companies abroad, or labor migration for an indefinite period of time. All of these are temporary migrations that only sometimes, as a result of long-term residence abroad, turn into permanent emigration.

As the above figures show, since the late nineteenth century, transatlantic emigration from Germany has decreased, while continental labor immigration into Germany has increased: at the end of the nineteenth century, the secular demographic and economic crisis caused by the disproportional growth of both population and labor force came to an end. During the rapid industrial growth of the two decades before World War I, labor shortage replaced the surplus of labor that previously had been the strongest demographic and economic motivation for transatlantic emigration. For this reason, since the 1890s continental immigration into Germany, particularly into Prussia, became a mass movement. As shown above, from 1880 until 1893 1.8 million Germans left their country; by 1913, however, there were already 1.2 million "foreign migrant workers" *(ausländische Wanderarbeiter)* in the German Reich. In Prussia, Poles from central Poland, at that time part of Russia, as well as Poles and Ruthenians from Austrian Galicia and Italians formed the main contingent of the labor force migrating into Germany (Bade 1980b, 348–77).

In Prussia in the 1880s and early 1890s, economic and political interests concerning the question of migrating labor came into conflict with one another. Employers, especially in the Prussian East, were interested in willing and cheap *(willig und billig)* foreign labor from across the eastern borders, while the Prussian government was afraid of political destabilization in the Polish-populated border regions of the east, where the national-revolutionary dream of a revival of the Polish state could not be suppressed. The basic idea of the Prussian defense policy *(Preussische Abwehrpolitik)* was therefore to fight against the "polonization of the East" *(Polonisierung des Ostens)* (Max Weber) that would result from immigration across Germany's eastern borders.

The conflict between economic and political interests was solved by the implementation of a system of compulsory rotation that limited labor immigration to seasonal employment. The result was a structure, similar to a temperature curve, showing the annual fluctuation of labor migration across the eastern borders to Prussia and back to the East: rapid rise in springtime, summit during the height of the summer, and sharp decline at the beginning of the restrictive period in the winter. Foreign workers from the East were welcomed in spring, but they had to leave Prussian territory before Christmas to avoid deportation. These problems scarcely affected rural employers. Industrial and commercial employers, however, struggled, largely in vain, to get special permission to employ Polish labor without seasonal limitations (Bade 1980c, 273–99; 1984a, 91–162; 1984b, 163–283).

In the central and western provinces of Prussia, with the exception of agricultural work, strictly controlled employment prohibition was imposed on Poles from abroad in order to avoid a second ethnonationalist fear: the "polonization of the West" *(Polonisierung des Westens).* In the Prussian West, a region dominated by coal and steel industries, there was a growing fear that Polish immigrants would join the Prussian "Ruhr Poles," ethnic Poles mostly from the Prussian East. Since the "Ruhr Poles" were Prussian citizens and not foreigners, they could not be prevented from internal east-to-west migration, but their rights as citizens were restricted in many ways (Klessmann 1978).

The Prussian Defense Policy was aimed only at the Polish majority of labor migrants in the east of Prussia. Nevertheless, in Prussia as well as in the German federal states that adopted the Prussian concept, all other foreign labor migrants were subject to this control system. While migrations of Poles from abroad were strictly regulated by this system, migrations of other foreign labor were only observed, not regulated. Italian labor migrants, for instance, were free to move within the labor market even in the Prussian Ruhr area, although their movements, too, fluctuated considerably (Del Fabbro 1996; Wennemann 1997).

In the Weimar Republic, the admission of foreigners no longer depended on the security principles of the Prussian Defense Policy but rather on the economic ratio of labor market policy: foreign laborers were only admitted if their employers could prove that no German workers were available. This new system, called "license requirement" *(Genehmigungspflicht)*, was based on the model of public labor administration *(öffentliche Arbeitsverwaltung)* developed during World War I. The employment of foreign labor in the Weimar Republic remained low, and in pre-World War II Germany it increased only slowly until 1938. This was mainly the result of restrictive foreign exchange policies impeding the transfer of wages in Nazi Germany (Bade 1980a, 160–87).

After the outbreak of World War II, foreign labor was replaced by the slavery of millions of deported foreign workers *(Fremdarbeiter)* and prisoners of war, a method the Nazi war economy called the deployment of foreigners *(Ausländereinsatz)*. After the war, victims of this policy accounted for the majority of Displaced Persons (DPs), amounting to about 12 million people in occupied Germany. One decade later, in the middle of the 1950s, the hiring of "guest workers" *(Gastarbeiter)* opened a new chapter of employment of foreigners in Germany, which, to some extent, adopted the traditions of the Weimar Republic (Herbert 1986, 120–236).

Public Discussion and National Policies

Since transatlantic emigration had become a social mass movement in the first half of the nineteenth century, the public and governmental activities concerning the emigration question were shaped by two main issues: on the one hand, humanitarian and charitable motives, and, on the other, ideological intentions. Both perspectives were highly complex, with often overlapping arguments. The public discussion of these issues climaxed in the 1840s and 1880s.

Part of the debate regarding humanity and charity in the middle of the century (Fenske 1973, 221–36) included private counseling efforts for prospective emigrants and appeals for governmental protection of emigrants. There were numerous private emigration clubs in the 1830s and 1840s—groups whose efforts often failed, with disastrous consequences for the emigrants—and a broad public debate on emigration questions. The emigration law acknowledged by the Frankfurt National Assembly in 1849 represented the climax of the endeavors to gain governmental commitment. This law, which would have created a central migration office with the status of a national ministry, aimed to achieve unlimited freedom of emigration, to protect emigrants and Germans abroad, to eliminate nonlicensed migration agents, and to inspect the emigrants' ships. The revolution failed, and the emigration law as well as the emigration office remained revolutionary dreams (Kuckhoff 1976, 102–45).

The ideological discussion of migration issues at midcentury was informed by efforts to influence, control, and organize migration, that is, to take advantage of the phenomenon especially for socioeconomic purposes. Criticisms pointed to the cultural bleeding *(Aderlass),* the loss of human capital, and to persons avoiding conscription, while proponents simultaneously favored emigration as a means to alleviate social problems, partly by "exporting" poor people and criminals. More important in this context was the idea of using transatlantic emigration as a "social safety valve" to void revolutionary elements. This idea became a central focus of the emigration debate throughout the nineteenth century, although it never led to regular public programs (Hansen 1976, 8–61; Moltmann 1984, 272–97).

Research into the degree to which emigration actually may have served these functions has only begun. For many emigrants, departure was a gesture of nonviolent social protest against the living conditions in their homeland. Perhaps if millions of Germans had not had the opportunity to emigrate in the nineteenth century and the majority of those who stayed had not been able to dream of the New World as a real and viable alternative, the expectation of Karl Marx and Friedrich Engels that the lost political revolution of 1848/49 would be followed by a successful social revolution might not have turned out to be simply a false projection.

In the second half of the nineteenth century, the discussion of emigration reached another plateau as the question about colonial expansion arose in the late 1870s and early 1880s. The public debate was provoked anew in 1879 by the propaganda pamphlet "Does Germany Need Colonies?" written by Friedrich Fabri, the director of the Rhenish Missionary Society and the leading German expansion publicist. Partly following the ideas of Wakefield and Torrens and reviving points of the midcentury public debate, Fabri's book concentrated on questions of population and emigration. His argument was reinforced by the renewed vigor of transatlantic emigration in the early 1880s. The public debate stimulated by Fabri's book and the ensuing publications by other authors combined nationalistic visions and ethnocultural ideas with economic calculations and social imperialist strategies (Bade 1975).

During the crisis-prone and hectic transition from an agricultural to an industrial society, emigration was still considered to be a sociopolitical necessity *(sozialpolitische Notwendigkeit)* in order to reduce the danger of social revolution. However, there was a simultaneous desire to preserve the "Germanness" *(Deutschtum)* of the immigrants and to avoid the loss of human capital, especially to the competing power of the U.S. economy in the world market. For this reason, theoreticians argued that emigration should be directed from North to South America or to the German colonies still to be acquired. This was justified through ideological theorems of ethnocultural "amalgamation" and "resistance": there was fear that German emigrants would be quickly absorbed into the civilization and economy of the New World because of the cultural relationship of the German and North American civilizations and the superiority and attractiveness of the New World's economy. By directing immigrants to South America, which, it was suggested, was culturally and economically inferior, and to the German colonies, it was hoped that the emigrants would maintain their "Germanness," remaining attached to their home country's culture as well as to its economy. This would not only support the "Germanness" of the settlers, but it would also increase exports from the "mother country" by creating new markets linked by ethnocultural bonds of loyalty and excluding foreign competition. These ambitions, it was hoped, would transform the deplorable ethnocultural and economic "disadvantages" of "sociopolitically necessary emigration" into "advantages" for the Reich. Finally, it was believed, emigration would become unnecessary because of the economic growth at home that would follow the opening of new overseas markets (Bade 1975, 80–99, 354–60).

All these plans and hopes remained unfulfilled. On the one hand, the propaganda for establishing German districts had a somewhat negative effect on South American countries' attitudes toward immigration from Germany. In Brazil, for example, an informal German state within the Brazilian state was regarded with suspicion, and benefit programs for German immigrants were temporarily suspended while other groups of immigrants, especially Italians, were steered into the German settlement areas (Luebke 1987, 1–82). On the other hand, emigration on the whole could not be controlled or even directed. Finally, the protectorates *(Schutzgebiete)* of the German Colonial Empire in Africa and the Pacific region, founded in 1884/85 and lost during World War I, were absolutely unsuited for mass immigration. Moreover, already in the early 1890s, German transatlantic emigration as a social mass movement had come to an end (Bade 1983a, 91–108; cf. Bade 1989b, 183–215).

As had been the case in the public debate of the 1840s, the discussion on emigration during the late 1870s and the early 1880s again called for migration legislation. The mass movement, however, was mostly left to itself: in the USA restrictive quota legislation had as yet not been passed and in Germany there had been no further state restrictions imposed on emigration since the early nineteenth century. The migration legislation of the German states was liberal, and, as mentioned above, their migration policies—as far as they had them—were fueled in part by the idea of exporting social problems overseas.

Actually, a German emigration legislation as such could not have been enacted before the founding of the German Reich. The protection of the emigrants formed an exception: shocking accounts of disastrous conditions on board the emigration ships led to the appointment of a federal commissioner (later on, Reich's commissioner) for emigration affairs *(Bundes-/Reichskommissar für das Auswanderungswesen)* in 1869. This official's duty was to control emigration, particularly to inspect the emigrants' ships in Hamburg and Bremen, to report grievances, and to ask local authorities for corrective measures. Apart from that, governmental involvement in emigration questions was limited to various internal regulations issued by individual German states. These rules were designed especially to control foreign emigration agents and to prevent the emigration of people dodging military service (von Hippel 1984; Schöberl 1990; Bretting and Bickelmann 1991).

The constitution of the German Reich of 1871 (art. 4, no. 1) conferred the responsibility for emigration issues to the Reich itself. However, during the early years of the empire Bismarck and the agrarian-conservative political elite in the German Reich refused to consider an emigration law. This was odd, given the general shift from liberalism to protectionism and state intervention, visible, for example, in the forms of welfare legislation, protective duties against foreign trade competition, and overseas protectorates. Nevertheless, the belief was that a legislative pursuit of emigration issues would mean official acknowledgment of the subject and even support for a mass phenomenon that was unpopular, especially among agrarian employers. This was true particularly in the Prussian East, for the predominant contingent of the mass emigration of the 1880s came from the largely agrarian northeast regions of the Reich, where there was already a growing shortage of labor.

More than a quarter of a century after the founding of the German Empire, the legislative responsibility of the Reich established in 1871 was finally applied to questions of emigration. The first Reich Emigration Law (Reichsauswanderungsgesetz) became effective in 1897, when mass emigration from nineteenth-century Germany had already been a thing of the past for several years. Consequently, the law concentrated largely on the protection of German emigrants and contained only a few indirect mechanisms for controlling emigration by consulting emigrants and granting licenses to emigration agencies and shipping lines. In 1902 a Central Enquiry Office for Emigrants was opened to give advice to emigrants. Supervised by the chancellor of the empire, it was not a governmental office but assigned instead to the German Colonial Society. This was an expression of a vain hope that at least part of the stream of overseas emigration might be diverted toward the colonies (Langbein and Henning 1989, 292–301).

While the national state clearly lacked interest in emigration questions, from the beginning there had been, as already mentioned, a strong commitment to continental immigration, which was subject to the policies of the individual German federal states. This interest was of Prussian origin as the strongest contingents of continental immigration were coming across the eastern Prussian borders. In spite of many differences of opinion at the governmental level and in the legislation and administration of the individual German states, the general intentions and tendencies toward the questions of transnational migration were twofold: to protect German transatlantic emigration and to protect Germany from continental immigration.

As discussed by Rogers Brubaker (1992), this matter can be related to the path from ethnocultural to ethnonational self-consciousness and the consequent strengthening of the jus sanguinis (the principle of ethnic heritage) tradition, codified in the citizenship law of 1913. The Prussian-German state of the nineteenth century had already established the general validity of jus sanguinis, and while ethnonational intentions first grew gradually, after the late nineteenth century they expanded rapidly in accordance with the principle. Jus sanguinis placed the principles of nation and national community above those of civil rights and republic, in strict opposition to the principle of territory (jus soli) embodied in the French republican idea. In addition to binding civil rights to the principle of ethnic descent, the law of 1913 aimed to prolong German citizenship for German emigrants and to limit the acquisition of German citizenship by foreigners to exceptional cases (114–32).

During World War I, for the first time, there were thoughts of a migration office to deal with the problems of transnational migration, for enormous migration movements were expected for the period after the war. In addition to continental labor immigration, strong movements of transnational emigration as well as continental remigration were anticipated. In particular, a heavy influx of remigration of Russian-Germans was anticipated, the result of the laws enforcing the liquidation of German property in Russia, which had already led to the ruin and expulsion of approximately 200,000 colonists from Wolhynia in 1915/16. In 1919 these considerations led to the foundation of the Reich Office for German Immigration, Remigration, and Emigration (Reichsamt für deutsche Einwanderung, Rückwanderung und Auswanderung), officially called the Reich Migration Office (Reichswanderungsamt) (Bickelmann 1980, 81–119; Thalheim 1926, 111–39; Bade 1989a, 312–21).

The transnational movements during the immediate postwar period, however, proved to be of less volume and duration than expected. Economic measures to consolidate the national budget meant therefore that the new Reich Migration Office was reduced to a Reich Emigration Agency (Reichsstelle für das Auswanderungswesen). The agency offered consulting programs to emigrants and vainly tried to change their minds. It was thus referred to in the contemporary debate as the "Reich Agency for Prevention" (Reichsverhinderungsamt) and the "Agency of lost words" (Amt der verlorenen Worte). In its reduced form and function, it survived the decline of the Weimar Republic. In Nazi Germany, it advised Jewish emigrants especially, leading to several conflicts with the Gestapo, but its final dissolution did not come until 1944 (Bickelmann 1980, 85–91; Kampe 1989, 326–35).

The ambiguous position of Germany as a country of transatlantic emigration as well as of continental labor immigration led to a unique ambivalence that became readily apparent in the Weimar Republic. As an emigration country, Germany opposed the increasing international protective restrictions against immigration, especially those of the USA, which was the main destination for German immigrants. As a labor-importing country *(Arbeitseinfuhrland)* (Ferenczi 1921, 898–904), however, Germany had to defend its own system for controlling continental immigration. With regard to protective intentions, in fact, the German system was comparable to U.S. policy toward immigration.

This dual role also determined the German attitude toward multilateral endeavors by the international organizations developed after World War I to regulate emigration and immigration movements. Following the proposal of the International Labor Conference in Washington in 1919, there were attempts to fashion bilateral treaties with the European nations that were sources of foreign migrant labor in Germany. During multilateral negotiations concerning the regulation of international migrations in the 1920s, however, the German position vacillated, depending on whether regulation under consideration affected the country of emigration or the "labor-importing country." This variability was characteristic of both government representatives and those representing organized interests on the labor market.

Attempts to regulate migration began with the Central European economic conference on the organization of the labor market, held in Budapest in 1910, and continued during the meeting of the delegates of the emigration countries, in Rome in 1921; the first international conference of emigration and immigration countries, in Rome in 1924; the World Migration Convention, organized in London in 1926 by the International Federation of Trade Unions and the Labor and Socialist International; and, finally, the second international conference of emigration and immigration countries, held in 1928 in Havana. To this last conference Germany sent only one observer, who did not have permission to enter the discussion or to vote.

The first conference in Rome, which was promising, was followed by the disappointing one in Havana. The general impression of the Havana participants was that negotiations on problems of emigration and immigration should be addressed to the International Labor Office rather than to conferences organized by the emigration and immigration countries themselves. Both the International Commission of Emigration, already established in 1920 by the International Labor Organization, and the Permanent Emigration Committee in Geneva, however, were affected by the conflicting intentions of emigration and immigration countries (Willcox 1969; cf. Bade 1980a).

Transnational migration in the era of National Socialism was characterized by neither continuity nor discontinuity. In fact, existing continuities were augmented gradually and eventually aggravated and distorted almost beyond recognition in a process that culminated during World War II. What resulted was a new dimension different in quality yet still representing a continuity: on the one hand, after 1933 efforts were being made to influence Germans abroad by the ideas of National Socialism and encourage them to remigrate "home" to National Socialist Germany. On the other hand, the persecution of many Germans for political, religious, and racist reasons pushed them into exile that often led to permanent emigration. As regards citizenship, the consequences of national socialist "Germanness" policies resulted, for many people, in humiliation, deprivation of all rights, and finally the stripping away of civil rights; Jews, especially, branded as "ethnic aliens" *(Fremdvölkische)*, were victim-ized. As long as the borders remained open there was a chance to escape by emigration. After the borders were sealed, the road finally led to the organized mass murder of the Holocaust. For continental immigration, the road led from the employment of foreign migrant labor to the unlimited exploitation of slave labor brought into the Reich especially from East European territo-ries (Herbert 1985, 1991).

Contradictory approaches to dealing with the problems of transnational migration continued in Germany after World War II. As in the 1920s, the German position remained determined by the ambivalent tension between protecting emigrants from Ger-many and protecting Germany from true immigration. The pro-tection of emigrants—one instrument for which was the Decree against Unacceptable Conditions in Emigration (Verordnung gegen Mißstände im Auswanderungswesen) of 1924—was contin-ued in the Federal Republic by the establishment of the Federal Emigration Agency (Bundesstelle für das Auswanderungswesen), which in 1950 even employed people previously connected to the Reich Emigration Agency (1924–1944), and in 1952 was renamed the Federal Emigration Office (Bundesamt für Auswanderung). Another legislative continuity relates to the protection of emi-grants, which culminated in 1975, when a law intended to protect emigrants from exploitation, deprivation of rights, and misrepre-sentation was passed. All of this was part of a long tradition that had begun in 1869 with the appointment by the North German League of the federal commissioner for emigration affairs in the North German League (Frieler and Henning 1989).

In 1959/60, the Federal Emigration Office was integrated into the Federal Administration Office (Bundesverwaltungsamt). The new office was to deal with questions and problems related to emigration as well as to immigration; however, it mainly con-centrated on emigration issues. It seems to be largely unknown in public debate that the constitution of the FRG (Grundgesetz/ GG) includes the responsibility for emigration legislation (Art. 73, ¶3 GG) and that the 1959 founding law (Errichtungsgesetz) of the Federal Administration Office (Art. 2, ¶3) clearly states that the office may perform the same duties in the fields of both immigration and emigration. This means, in fact, that the nec-essary administrative body to take action on immigration issues has already been established by law, while an immigration law is still nonexistent. Although in view of the above the establishment of an immigration law would not require a constitutional amendment, the willingness to rethink migration policy is gaining ground only at a very slow pace (Bade 1994b, 95f.).

So far, the Federal Administration Office deals only informally with immigration issues in the context of the immigration and integration of accepted ethnic Germans from East and Southeast Europe *(Aussiedler)*. These, however, are not considered immigrants but Germans according to German law (Art. 116 GG, Bundesvertriebenen- und Flüchtlingsgesetz, Kriegsfolgenbereinigungsgesetz). German legislation states that minorities of German descent in Eastern Europe and other regions farther east, where many descendants of Germans were settled following deportation from the former Volga Republic in 1941, are still suffering from post-World War II "expulsion pressure" *(Vertreibungsdruck)*. The preconditions to being accepted for return to Germany as an *Aussiedler* are German descent and the "confession of Germanness" *(Bekenntnis zum Deutschtum)*.[1]

The legal right of the descendants of Germans who had emigrated generations before to return to the homeland of their ancestors as "Germans" is grounded in the jus sanguinis tradition and in an ethnocultural and ethnonational understanding of German identity. The policy toward ethnic Germans from Eastern Europe *(Aussiedlerpolitik)*, however, works like an informal immigration policy following ethnic criteria and, in addition, is said to be a kind of peaceful German contribution to an "ethnic purge" *(ethnische Säuberung)* (Olt 1994; Bade 1994a, 25–8, 147–74). A similar continuity is visible in the defensive attitudes opposing regular immigration legislation and policies, which undoubtedly need to shift from the pure jus sanguinis principle as a basis for immigration and citizenship to a new principle that would embrace elements of both jus sanguinis and jus soli.

Migration as Profit and Loss in the German Postwar States

The ambivalent attitude toward emigration and immigration issues has hardly changed in postwar Germany, although a shift

in emphasis from emigration to immigration issues has accelerated dramatically since World War II. More than in any other
Western industrial state during the second half of this century,
the population, economy, and society in West Germany have
been characterized by mass migration movements. Since World
War II, three large integration processes can be distinguished in
Germany: the integration of refugees and expellees in West and
East Germany; the development from the "foreign labor recruitment," via the resulting "guest-worker question," to the true
immigration problem in West Germany; and, finally, the new
integration issue facing the united Germany of the early 1990s
(see the next section). The different and partly contradictory
experiences of West and East Germans with migration and with
the encounters between domestic and immigration populations
finally influenced the encounter of East and West Germans
themselves during the unification process.

The first important integration issue was the integration
of refugees and expellees from the former German East and
from East European regions. In West Germany, they were
called "expellees from home" *(Heimatvertriebene),* whereas in
East Germany they were euphemistically called "resettlers"
(Umsiedler). What influential expellee organizations in the West
publicly referred to for decades as the "legal claim to return"
(Recht auf Heimat) remained taboo in the GDR, whose leaders
did not want to attract the attention of their eastern neighbors
and therefore quietly referred to a "resettlement problem"
(Umsiedlerproblematik).

The integration of refugees and expellees (resettlers) aside,
until the construction of the Berlin Wall in 1961 and to a lesser
degree afterward, out-migration, flight, and finally legal reloca-
tion to the west *(Übersiedlung)*—rather than immigration and
integration—were predominant issues in the GDR. For West
Germany, the influx from East Germany was characterized as
"flight from the Communist sphere of influence" *(Flucht aus dem
kommunistischen Machtbereich).* It therefore was politically
accepted and indeed welcomed as a needed boost to the labor
force. In the GDR, however, out-migration—as a rule illegal since
1961—was a criminal act called "flight from the republic"
(Republikflucht) and was hushed up in public discussion, as had
been the so-called resettlement problem since the early 1950s.

Consequently, in East Germany many immigration, integration, emigration, and exclusion issues were publicly repressed and became political taboos (Heidemeier 1994; Ackermann 1996).

In the West, many German expellees and refugees were still strangers in their new home country when the officially organized foreign labor recruitment began with the German-Italian Treaty of 1955. This recruitment marked the onset of the second large integration process in the West. The building of the Wall in 1961 brought the influx from the GDR to a halt and precipitated West Germany's reluctant move toward becoming a country of immigration. The recruitment of foreign labor from then on increased dramatically. However, there was no comprehensive and long-term concept in the Federal Republic for dealing with the permanent integration of the immigrated foreign labor population and the resulting social problems. For decades, "policy concerning foreigners" *(Ausländerpolitik)* was largely limited to labor market politics applied to foreigners, only later coming to include cautious attempts to foster the "temporary social integration" *(soziale Integration auf Zeit)* of foreigners.

The guest-worker period in West Germany ended in 1973 with a labor recruitment stop *(Anwerbestop)*. This had a boomerang effect on German policy toward foreigners: the number of foreigners decreased for only a short time, while, by lowering the transnational fluctuation of the foreign migrant labor force, the already growing tendency toward permanent residence was strengthened. Foreign workers who were not willing to live permanently separated from their families were left with only two possibilities: either to return to their home country without a chance of being readmitted into Germany later or to stay and have their families move to Germany. Most of them chose the latter solution, and by 1979 the number of foreigners in Germany exceeded the figure of 1973, in part as a result of families moving to Germany but also because of the natural growth of the foreign population within the German borders.

The appeal of staying typically grew with the length of residence. Thus "guest workers" gradually evolved into immigrants. At the beginning of the 1980s, a significant and growing part of this foreign minority made up of the former "guest-worker" population lived in the FRG in the paradoxical position of being de facto immigrants in a country that did not consider itself an immigration country. The government of the FRG, however, consistently denied that Germany was inevitably becoming a country of immigration. It suppressed political action regarding immigration thereby foreclosing any political discussion and administrative handling of the issue. As long as true immigration is a taboo subject, policies toward immigration cannot be developed. The formulation of a framework for handling immigration and integration issues is long overdue.

To a small extent, foreign workers were also employed in the GDR on the basis of interstate agreements. This employment was officially hushed up or played down as "training migration" *(Ausbildungswanderung)* although the "foreign workers" *(ausländische Werktätige)* in the East—like the "guest workers" in the West—were employed under the hardest conditions and in jobs Germans liked least of all (e.g., three-quarters of the foreigners worked shifts). In the GDR, there was administrative, patriarchal "care" for foreign workers, but on the whole there was more state-prescribed separation and less social integration of foreign labor than in the FRG. Foreign workers in the GDR were often quartered in separate mass accommodations that kept them socially at a distance. In this social vacuum created by state-sponsored segregation, a latent xenophobia began to grow that erupted at the end of the GDR's existence.

During the unification process, it became evident that the two groups of Germans, with their opposing political, ideological, and personal experiences, had become strangers to one another. Among other things, they had to address the unsolved problems regarding the treatment of foreigners in both states, and they had to deal with the shadows of German history, particularly in this field (Bade 1994a, 38–90; cf. Grundmann et al. 1991, 6–75; Krüger-Potratz 1991).

"Native Foreigners" and "Foreign Germans" in the Unification Process

The new integration issue attending the unification process of the early 1990s was much more complicated than both of the preceding post-World War II integration movements. Several very diverse groups of immigrants were involved, among them "native foreigners" *(einheimische Ausländer)*, or "foreign inlanders" *(ausländische Inländer)*, as well as "strange Germans" *(fremde Deutsche):*

1. The largest minority group has been and still is composed of three generations of "native foreigners" or "foreign inlanders" originating from the former "guest-worker" population, whose first generation is already entering retirement.

2. The ethnic Germans from the East *(Aussiedler)*, with more than 200,000 immigrating each year since the late 1980s, make up the second largest group. These "foreign Germans" are coming from former communist countries, and although they are legally Germans, they are in most cases confronted with all the heavy psychological and mental pressures of actual immigration, which are sometimes severe enough to lead them to remigrate.

3. Since the early 1980s, the number of refugees and asylum seekers—coming from the so-called third world up to the mid-1980s and mostly from Eastern Europe today—has grown considerably. The new restrictive asylum law of 1993, while decreasing the number of applications for asylum, has probably increased the number of illegal residents. The most recent group of immigrants to Germany are Jews from the former Soviet Union. In addition to immigrations crossing German borders, there were in the early 1990s two big inter-German integration issues caused by people moving across borders and borders moving across people.

    a. People crossing borders: In West Germany, those numerous Germans who, until the late 1980s, traveled as refugees from the GDR to the supposedly golden West and those who went to the West during the unification process *(Übersiedler)* had—and partly still have—identity problems to overcome. Many of them suffer a German-German culture shock caused by the differences in material culture and mentality between the communist East and the capitalist West.

    b. Borders moving across people: East Germany faced not only economic and social but also mental integration problems during the unification process. Many people lived in a sort of imported integration situation, not because they had moved to foreign countries but because of alienation at home. During the rapid process of social, economic, and political transformation in the early 1990s, many people, now strangers in their own land, faced two alternatives: conformity to Western ways without reservation or progressive alienation.

The problems and difficulties related to this increasing alienation process have reduced the willingness of many people in East Germany to accept and integrate foreigners, including asylum seekers assigned to the five new federal states according to the Unification Treaty. The sense of alienation at home has increasingly led to defensive attitudes and hostility toward foreigners, and violent attacks were already occurring prior to the well-publicized violence in Saxon Hoyerswerda in September 1991. Much like the offenses against foreigners that had occurred in the West, the earlier violence in the East was hardly noticed because the media had not yet latched on to this new phenomenon. At first, the growing hostility toward foreigners was more aggressive and violent in the East, but on the whole, it has turned out neither to be typically East German nor caused solely by social fringe groups threatened by social decline. Rather, it has found fertile ground in the West and increasingly has enveloped all of unified Germany (Bade 1994b, 175–206; cf. Bukow and Llaryora 1993; Dietz and Hilkes 1994).

Since 1991, names of German towns where violent offenses have taken place have become catchwords worldwide for xenophobic terror. In Hoyerswerda (17–22 September 1991) in the East, for example, asylum seekers were driven out of their homes, attacked on public buses, and injured by stones. In Rostock-Lichtenhagen in the East (23–27 August 1992), crowds applauded as asylum seekers were besieged and attacked in their homes and their houses were set afire. In Hünxe (10 October 1991) in the West, two refugee children were seriously injured during an arson attack. In Mölln (11 November 1992) and in Solingen (29 May 1993) in the West, members of Turkish families who were either long-term residents of Germany or born in Germany were burned to death in their homes or escaped with serious injuries. A synagogue was burnt in Lübeck during the night between 24 March and 25 March 1994, the first such attack in Germany since the November 1938 Nazi pogrom against the Jews. This was followed by other violent offenses in May 1995 and by letter-bomb attacks perpetrated by Austrian neo-Nazis that spread to Germany as well in mid-1995.

The riots in May and June 1993 at the scene of the Solingen murders and in other towns demonstrated the increasing readiness of victims of xenophobia to defend themselves, if necessary by going on the offensive. This is especially true for the young German Turks. Clearly, ethnosocial tension is growing. In addition, potential conflicts among foreigners are spreading to Germany from other countries. In one such instance, German authorities reacted to threats of violence by the Kurdistan Labor Party (PKK) by banning this and several other Kurdish organizations. This led to new problems because it is often difficult to make legal distinctions between the political and ethnocultural actions of more or less organized immigrant minority groups. The dilemma could no longer be ignored after the bloody Kurd demonstrations in March 1994, which were not only an ethnocultural protest against the prohibited celebration of the Kurdish New Year in Germany but also a celebration of the PKK and, at the same time, a political protest against the oppression of the Kurd minority in Turkey.

The new German xenophobia of the early 1990s, however, broadcast all over the world, was neither fascist nor distinctly German; xenophobia has also existed for a long time in other European countries of immigration. But Germany is something of a special case, since the new hostility toward minorities in united Germany and the excesses in German streets recall a history different from that of the rest of Europe.

The dark shadow of German history and the sensationalism of the media's coverage of right-wing extremism and violence against foreigners, however, has led to distortions and misinterpretations. Normal peaceful coexistence in united Germany is overlooked, as are all the countermovements and helpful initiatives, including the famous human chains of candles in the winter of 1992, the vast numbers of organized and spontaneous offers of help in daily life, the taking in and care of refugees, and the provision of hiding places for asylum seekers whose applications have been denied and who are to be deported. About 440,000 refugees claimed asylum in Germany in 1992. Moreover, Germany took in the bulk of refugees from the former Yugoslavia, accounting for about 320,000 in 1995: more than in all the other EC countries together (Willems et al. 1993).

The German Paradox: Immigration Country without Immigration Policies

The primary problems of immigration, integration, and minority issues and their social and political treatment have been mentioned only peripherally in many national and international discussions of the new German xenophobia. This is especially remarkable as the continued political disorientation of the population with regard to social problems and political tasks relating to immigration, integration, and minorities must be seen as an important source of the defensive attitudes toward foreigners.

The main cause of this political disorientation was and still is the emphatic denial that the Federal Republic in fact has become a new type of immigration country, not in a legal but in a social and cultural sense. The government continues to declare that "the Federal Republic is not an immigration country." Officially, Bonn still invokes the term "policy concerning foreigners" *(Ausländerpolitik),* rather than "immigration policy," when it responds to questions of immigration (Hoffmann 1990; Oberndörfer 1993).

The continuing reluctance to address immigration laws and politics can only be compared with the above-mentioned skepticism of Bismarck and leading agrarian and conservative circles in the Kaiserreich about the legitimization of emigration in the late nineteenth century. This attitude was based on the belief that an emigration law would only encourage emigration out of agricultural areas, which were already suffering from a labor shortage. It contributed to the fact that the first emigration law came too late, in 1897.

This delay, however, was not very important to the emigration countries, because the law served mainly to protect the emigrants, millions of whom were already living overseas, 90 percent of them in the United States. More then ten years ago, I wrote:

A delay in immigration legislation, however, could have disastrous consequences, not only for the fates of persons involved in the immigration process, but also for the immigration country as a whole, because the "de facto immigrants" are already in the country, yet as immigrants they remain outside the law as long as they cannot plan their lives with the help of laws regulating immigration and integration. There is a common mistake in which immigration legislation and immigration politics are confused with unlimited approval of immigration. If, in this context, a lesson may be learned from the history of emigration and immigration, it is the following one: immigration policy is not merely assistance to people who wish to immigrate. It is also a regulating instrument and therefore should be seen as a self-help for the country of immigration. (Bade 1983b, 122f.)

Warnings and hypotheses of this sort expressed in the early 1980s by researchers and people working with foreigners did not have any political consequences. In terms of migration and integration issues, the eventful 1980s were a lost decade. Meanwhile, the political and social scenario became more and more frightening: politicians denied the existence of problems that people were experiencing in everyday life. The paradoxical situation of immigration happening in a "nonimmigration country" has been, and still is, a peculiarly German type of multicultural reality.

The denial was the flipside of political helplessness and lack of guidelines governing immigration and integration affairs. Thus the increasing pressure exerted by the problems did not result only from the asylum hysteria of the 1980s and the early 1990s. It was primarily the result of earlier, more profound omissions concerning immigration issues. The asylum debate served merely to take people's minds off the larger issues. The price to pay for this became evident when, in the beginning of the 1990s, many additional problems arose as a result of the unification process. Among the population, a pervasive fear of foreigners was growing, while politicians began to fear citizens' attitudes toward foreigners as well as toward themselves.

Disorientation and fear among the population, coupled with the helplessness of politicians, had a decisive influence on the political credibility crisis, warnings of which had been sounded in vain for many years. For a brief period, this crisis even seemed to endanger the parliamentary democratic system. In autumn 1992 Chancellor Helmut Kohl spoke of a "national state of emergency" *(Staatsnotstand)* in migration affairs, which led some opinion leaders involved in the public debate to go so far as to recall the political instability, governmental powerlessness, and ultimate rejection of parliamentary democracy at the end of the Weimar Republic (Bade 1994a, 122).

In November 1993 sixty scholars issued *Das Manifest der 60*, a manifesto confronting the topic of "Germany and Immigration." According to these scholars, silent xenophobia, violent hostility toward strangers, and acceptance of violence in this context during the unification process of the early 1990s were "not inevitable consequences of immigration and integration, but rather avoidable results of the lack of political structuring of these processes" as well as "an aggressive response to the lack of migration policies" (Bade 1994c, 13, 20).

Today, Germany is facing the danger of a shift from alarmism to indifference. In the late 1980s and early 1990s political debate and the media coverage of asylum issues resulted in a sort of Titanic hysteria. In the election year of 1994, however, political parties and the media, fearing a resurrection of violent offenses against foreigners, avoided the explosive topics of migration, integration, and minorities.

In the end, there still remains the paradoxical issue of de facto immigration in a nonimmigration country. Currently there are some cautious attempts at structuring the issues with many open questions remaining for the future. But one thing is certain: migration policy cannot be limited to regulations for transnational movements fashioned with an eye to foreign security politics. It also requires corresponding internal policies for the integration of minorities. The internal side of migration politics thus falls essentially under the category of domestic social politics.

Such migration policies can only be successful if they are based on a large fundamental consensus. In a liberal democracy, any agreement must be carried by the will of the majority. A lack of widespread public support would lead to severe consequences from which both the immigrant minorities and the political system as a whole could suffer. Therefore migration policies must be properly promoted. Social coexistence, cultural tolerance, and social peace depend on whether and to what extent society, including the political elite in the united Germany, is willing to meet the challenges of migration through the development of comprehensive programs and farsighted perspectives (Cohn-Bendit and Schmid, 1992; Leggewie 1994, 55–60, 213–25; Schmalz-Jacobsen et al. 1993; Weidenfeld 1994).

In the wider context of immigration politics in Germany, two overlapping aspects of transatlantic movements have to be distinguished above all: flight and asylum, on the one hand, and labor migration and immigration, on the other. As to flight and asylum issues, the concerns and security of refugees must be taken care of, and in the countries of origin the causes for flight must be reduced as far as possible. Regarding labor migration and immigration, migration processes must be carefully regulated according to the receiving countries' own interests. Both aspects should be related to each other through comprehensive planning, but they must not be played off against each other in the public debate.

To handle all this while duly considering the interests of the countries of origin requires a migration-oriented development policy—or rather a development-oriented policy of migration. In this context, there is no avoiding an "international balance of burdens" (F. Nuscheler) to fight the global disasters that are creating mass migrations worldwide. At the same time, such a policy would be an important step in supporting sustainable growth as a guideline for economic, ecological, and social interventions aimed at creating an equitable and sustainable world that no longer lives on the credit of future generations (Hof 1993; Nuscheler 1995).

---

* Revised version of the opening address delivered at the first conference of the Joint German-American Project on Migration and Refugee Policies of the American Academy of Arts and Sciences, held 23–27 March 1995 in Cambridge, Massachusetts.

Notes

1. The law of 1993 substitutes the expression "fate of consequence of war" for the older "expulsion pressure."

References

Abel, Wilhelm. 1974. *Massenarmut und Hungerkrisen im vorindustriellen Europa: Versuch einer Synopsis.* Hamburg: Parey.

Ackermann, Volker. 1996. Der "echte" Flüchtling: Deutsche Vertriebene und Flüchtlinge aus der DDR, 1945–1961. Studien zur Historischen Migrationsforschung, vol. 1. Osnabrück: Universitätsverlag Rasch.

Bade, Klaus J. 1994a. *Ausländer—Aussiedler—Asyl: Eine Bestandsaufnahme.* Munich: Beck.

_____. 1994b. *Homo Migrans: Wanderungen aus und nach Deutschland—Erfahrungen und Fragen.* Essen: Klartext.

_____. 1989a, "Das 'Amt der verlorenen Worte': Das Reichswanderungsamt, 1918–1924." *Zeitschrift für Kulturaustausch* 39, no. 3: 312–21.

_____. 1989b. "Die 'zweite Reichsgründung' in Übersee: Imperiale Visionen, Kolonialbewegung und Kolonialpolitik in der Bismarckzeit." In *Die Herausforderung des europäischen Staatensystems: Nationale Ideologie und staatliches Interesse zwischen Restauration und Imperialismus*, ed. Adolf M. Birke and Günther Heydemann, 183–215. Göttingen: Vandenhoeck and Ruprecht.

_____. 1986. "Die deutsche überseeische Massenauswanderung im 19. und frühen 20. Jahrhundert: Bestimmungsfaktoren und Entwicklungsbedingungen." In *Auswanderer—Wanderarbeiter—Gastarbeiter: Bevölkerung, Arbeitsmarkt und Wanderung in Deutschland seit der Mitte des 19. Jahrhunderts*, ed. Klaus J. Bade, 1:259–99, 312–21. Ostfildern: Scripta Mercaturae.

_____. 1984a. "'Preussengänger' und 'Abwehrpolitik': Ausländerbeschäftigung, Ausländerpolitik und Ausländerkontrolle auf dem Arbeitsmarkt in Preussen vor dem Ersten Weltkrieg." *Archiv für Sozialgeschichte* 24: 91–162.

_____. 1983a. "Das Kaiserreich als Kolonialmacht: Ideologische Projektionen und historische Erfahrung." In *Die deutsche Frage im 19. und 20. Jahrhundert*, ed. Josef Becker and Andreas Hillgruber, 91–108. Munich: Vögel.

_____. 1983b. *Vom Auswanderungsland zum Einwanderungsland? Deutschland 1880 bis 1980*. Berlin: Colloquium.

_____. 1980a. "Arbeitsmarkt, Bevölkerung und Wanderung in der Weimarer Republik." In *Die Weimarer Republik—Belagerte Civitas*, ed. Michael Stürmer, 160–87. Königstein im Taunus: Athenäum.

_____. 1980b. "German Emigration to the United States and Continental Immigration to Germany, 1879–1979." *Central European History* 13, no. 4: 348–77.

_____. 1980c. "Politik und Ökonomie der Ausländerbeschäftigung im preussischen Osten: Die Internationalisierung des Arbeitsmarktes im 'Rahmen der preussischen Abwehrpolitik.'" In *Preussen im Rückblick*, ed. Hans-Jürgen Puhle and Hans-Ulrich Wehler, 273–99. Göttingen: Vandenhoeck and Ruprecht.

_____. 1975. *Friedrich Fabri und der Imperialismus in der Bismarckzeit: Revolution—Depression—Expansion*. Freiburg: Atlantis.

Bade, Klaus J., ed. 1994c. *Das Manifest der 60: Deutschland und die Einwanderung*. Munich: Beck.

_____. 1992. *Deutsche im Ausland—Fremde in Deutschland: Migration in Geschichte und Gegenwart*. Munich: Beck.

_____. 1987. *Population, Labour and Migration in Nineteenth and Twentieth Century Germany*. Leamington Spa: Berg.

_____. 1984b. "Arbeiterstatistik zur Ausländerkontrolle: Die 'Nachweisungen' der preussischen Landräte über den 'Zugang, Abgang und Bestand der ausländischen Arbeiter im preussischen Staate,' 1906–1914." *Archiv für Sozialgeschichte* 24: 163–283.

Benz, Wolfgang, ed. 1991. *Das Exil der kleinen Leute: Alltagserfahrungen deutscher Juden in der Emigration*. Munich: Beck.

Berliner Institut für Vergleichende Sozialforschung, ed. 1991. *Handbuch ethnischer Minderheiten in Deutschland*. Vol. 1. Berlin: Edition Parabolis.

Bethlehem, Siegfried. 1982. *Heimatvertreibung, DDR-Flucht, Gastarbeiterzuwanderung: Wanderungsströme und Wanderungspolitik in der Bundesrepublik Deutschland*. Stuttgart: Klett-Cotta.

Bickelmann, Hartmut. 1980. *Deutsche Überseeauswanderung in der Weimarer Zeit*. Wiesbaden: Steiner.

Brandes, Detlef. 1992. "Die Deutschen in Russland und der Sowjetunion." In *Deutsche im Ausland—Fremde in Deutschland: Migration in Geschichte und Gegenwart*, ed. Klaus J. Bade, 85–134. Munich: Beck.

Bretting, Agnes, and Hartmut Bickelmann. 1991. *Auswanderungsagenturen und Auswanderungsvereine im 19. und 20. Jahrhundert.* Stuttgart: Steiner.

Brubaker, Rogers. 1994. *Staats-Bürger: Deutschland und Frankreich im historischen Vergleich.* Hamburg: Junius.

———. 1992. *Citizenship and Nationhood in France and Germany.* Cambridge: Harvard University Press.

Bukow, Wolf-Dietrich, and Robert Llaryora. 1993. *Mitbürger aus der Fremde: Soziogenese ethnischer Minoritäten.* 2d ed. Opladen: Westdeutscher.

Cohn-Bendit, Daniel, and Thomas Schmid. 1992. *Heimat Babylon: Das Wagnis der multikulturellen Demokratie.* Hamburg: Hoffmann und Campe.

Del Fabbro, René. 1996. *Transalpini: Italienische Arbeitswanderung nach Süddeutschland im Kaiserreich, 1870/71–1918.* Studien zur Historischen Migrationsforschung, vol. 2. Osnabrück: Universitätsverlag Rasch.

Dietz, Barbara, and Peter Hilkes. 1994. *Integriert oder isoliert? Zur Situation russlanddeutscher Aussiedler in der Bundesrepublik Deutschland.* Munich: Olzog.

Dobert, Eitel Wolf. 1958. *Deutsche Demokraten in Amerika: Die Achtundvierziger und ihre Schriften.* Göttingen: Vandenhoeck and Ruprecht.

Doerries, Reinhard R. 1987. "German Transatlantic Migration from the Early Nineteenth Century to the Outbreak of World War II." In *Population, Labour and Migration in Nineteenth and Twentieth Century Germany,* ed. Klaus J. Bade, 115–34. Leamington Spa: Berg.

Dralle, Lothar. 1991. *Die Deutschen in Ostmittel- und Osteuropa: Ein Jahrtausend europäischer Geschichte.* Darmstadt: Wissenschaftliche Buchgesellschaft.

Fabri, Friedrich. 1879. *Bedarf Deutschland der Colonien? Eine politisch-ökonomische Betrachtung.* Gotha: Perthes.

Fenske, Hans. 1980. "International Migration: Germany in the Eighteenth Century." *Central European History* 13, no. 4: 332–47.

———. 1973. "Die deutsche Auswanderung in der Mitte des 19. Jahrhunderts: Öffentliche Meinung und amtliche Politik." *Geschichte in Wissenschaft und Unterricht* 24, no. 4: 221–36.

Ferenczi, Imre. 1929. "Proletarian Mass Migrations, Nineteenth and Twentieth Centuries." In *International Migrations,* vol. 1, *Statistics,* ed. Walter F. Willcox, 81ff. New York: National Bureau of Economic Research.

———. 1921. "Die internationale Regelung der Aus- und Einwanderung." *Soziale Praxis und Archiv für Volkswohlfahrt* 30: 898–904.

Focke, Harald. 1976. "Friedrich List und die südwestdeutsche Amerikaauswanderung, 1817–1846." In *Deutsche Amerikaauswanderung im 19. Jahrhundert: Sozialgeschichtliche Beiträge*, ed. Günter Moltmann, 63–100. Stuttgart: Metzler.

Frieler, Birgit, and Wiebke Henning. 1989. "Auswanderung nach 1945: Hoffnung für Millionen–Schutz und Fürsorge für Auswanderer als staatliche Aufgabe." *Zeitschrift für Kulturaustausch* 39, no. 3: 336–44.

Grundmann, Herbert, et al. 1991. "Ausländer in Ostdeutschland." *Wissenschaftliche Mitteilungen aus dem Berliner Institut für Sozialwissenschaftliche Studien* 3: 6–75.

Hansen, Christine. 1976. "Die deutsche Auswanderung im 19. Jahrhundert—ein Mittel zur Lösung sozialer und sozialpolitischer Probleme?" In *Deutsche Amerikaauswanderung im 19. Jahrhundert: Sozialgeschichtliche Beiträge*, ed. Günter Moltmann, 8–61. Stuttgart: Metzler.

Heckmann, Friedrich. 1992. *Ethnische Minderheiten, Volk und Nation: Soziologie inter-ethnischer Beziehungen*. Stuttgart: Enke.

Heidemeier, Helge. 1994. *Flucht und Zuwanderung aus der SBZ/DDR, 1945/1949–1961: Die Flüchtlingspolitik der Bundesrepublik Deutschland bis zum Bau der Berliner Mauer*. Düsseldorf: Droste.

Helbich, Wolfgang, Walter D. Kamphoefner, and Ulrike Sommer, eds. 1988. *Briefe aus Amerika: Deutsche Auswanderer schreiben aus der Neuen Welt, 1830–1930*. Munich: Beck.

Herbert, Ulrich. 1986. *Geschichte der Ausländerbeschäftigung in Deutschland, 1880–1980: Saisonarbeiter—Zwangsarbeiter—Gastarbeiter*. Berlin: Dietz.

_____. 1985. *Fremdarbeiter: Politik und Praxis des "Ausländer-Einsatzes" in der Kriegswirtschaft des Dritten Reiches*. Berlin: Dietz.

Herbert, Ulrich, ed. 1991. *Europa und der "Reichseinsatz": Ausländische Zivilarbeiter, Kriegsgefangene und KZ-Häftlinge in Deutschland, 1938–1945*. Essen: Klartext.

Hippel, Wolfgang von. 1984. *Auswanderung aus Südwestdeutschland: Studien zur württembergischen Auswanderung und Auswanderungspolitik im 18. und 19. Jahrhundert*. Stuttgart: Klett-Cotta.

Hof, Bernd. 1993. *Europa im Zeichen der Migration: Szenarien zur Bevölkerungs- und Arbeitsmarktentwicklung in der Europäischen Gemeinschaft bis 2020*. Cologne: Deutscher Instituts-Verlag.

Hoffmann, Lutz. 1994. *Das deutsche Volk und seine Feinde: Die völkische Droge—Aktualität und Entstehungsgeschichte*. Cologne: PapyRossa.

_____. 1990. *Die unvollendete Republik: Zwischen Einwanderungsland und deutschem Nationalstaat.* Cologne: PapyRossa.

Kampe, Nobert. 1989. "Die Reichsstelle für das Auswanderungswesen und die Vertreibung der Juden, 1933–1941." *Zeitschrift für Kulturaustausch* 39, no. 3: 326–35.

Kamphoefner, Walter D. 1980. "Dreissiger and Forty-Eighters: The Political Influence of Two Generations of German Political Exiles." In *Germany and America: Essays on Problems of International Relations and Immigrations*, ed. Hans L. Trefousse, 89–102. New York: Brooklyn College Press.

Klessmann, Christoph. 1978. *Polnische Bergarbeiter im Ruhrgebiet: Soziale Integration und nationale Subkultur einer Minderheit in der deutschen Industriegesellschaft.* Göttingen: Vandenhoeck and Ruprecht.

Krüger-Potratz, Marianne, ed. 1991. *Anderssein gab es nicht: Ausländer und Minderheiten in der DDR.* Münster: Waxmann.

Kuckhoff, Michael. 1976. "Die Auswanderungsdiskussion während der Revolution von 1848/49." In *Deutsche Amerikaauswanderung im 19. Jahrhundert: Sozialgeschichtliche Beiträge*, ed. Günter Moltmann, 102–45. Stuttgart: Metzler.

Labrousse, Camille Ernest. 1932. *Esquisse du mouvement des prix et des revenus en France au dix-huitième siècle.* Paris: Librairie Dalloz.

Labrousse, Ernest. 1943. *La crise de l'économie française à la fin de l'ancien régime et au début de la révolution.* Paris: Presses universitaires de France.

Langbein, Ralph, and Wiebke Henning. 1989. "Staat und Auswanderung im 19. Jahrhundert." *Zeitschrift für Kulturaustausch* 39, no. 3: 292–301.

Leggewie, Claus. 1994. "Das Ende der Lebenslügen: Plädoyer für eine neue Einwanderungspolitik." In *Das Manifest der 60: Deutschland und die Einwanderung*, ed. Klaus J. Bade, 55–60, 213–25. Munich: Beck.

Luebke, Frederick C. 1987. *Germans in Brazil: A Comparative History of Cultural Conflict During World War I.* Baton Rouge: Louisiana State University Press.

Moltmann, Günter. 1986. "The Migration of German Redemptioners to North America, 1720–1820." In *Colonialism and Migration: Indentured Labour before and after Slavery*, ed. Pieter C. Emmer, 105–22. Dordrecht: Nijhoff.

_____. 1984. "Auswanderung als Revolutionsersatz?" In *Die Deutschen und die Revolution*, ed. Michael Salewski, 272–97. Göttingen: Muster-Schmidt.

_____, ed. 1982. *Germans to America: Three Hundred Years of Immigration, 1683–1983.* Stuttgart: Institut für Auslandsbeziehungen.

_____. 1979. *Aufbruch nach Amerika: Friedrich List und die Auswanderung aus Baden und Württemberg, 1816/17. Dokumentation einer sozialen Bewegung.* Tübingen: Wunderlich.

_____. 1976. *Deutsche Amerikaauswanderung im 19. Jahrhundert: Sozialgeschichtliche Beiträge.* Stuttgart: Metzler.

Nuscheler, Franz. 1995. *Internationale Migration, Flucht und Asyl.* Opladen: Leske and Budrich.

Oberndörfer, Dieter. 1993. *Der Wahn des Nationalen: Die Alternative der offenen Republik.* Freiburg im Breisgau: Herder.

Olt, R. 1994. "Zwischen Selbstpreisgabe und Hoffnung: Die Lage nationaler Minderheiten in Osteuropa." *Frankfurter Allgemeine Zeitung,* 28 Feb. 1994.

Röder, Werner, and Herbert A. Strauss, eds. 1980–83. *Internationales Biographisches Handbuch der deutschsprachigen Emigration nach 1933/International Biographical Dictionary of Central European Emigrés, 1933–1945,* 3 vols. Munich: Saur.

Rosenberg, Hans. 1974. *Die Weltwirtschaftskrise, 1857–1859.* 2d ed. Göttingen: Vandenhoeck and Ruprecht.

Schmalz-Jacobsen, Cornelia, Holger Hinte, and Georgios Tsapanos. 1993. *Einwanderung—und dann? Perspektiven einer neuen Ausländerpolitik.* Munich: Knaur.

Schmalz-Jacobsen, Cornelia, and Georg Hansen, eds. 1995. *Ethnische Minderheiten in der Bundesrepublik Deutschland: Ein Lexikon.* Munich: Beck.

Schöberl, Ingrid. 1990. *Amerikanische Einwandererwerbung in Deutschland, 1845–1914.* Stuttgart: Steiner.

Thalheim, Karl C. 1926. *Das deutsche Auswanderungsproblem der Nachkriegszeit.* Jena: Gustav Fischer.

Weidenfeld, Werner, ed. 1994. *Das europäische Einwanderungskonzept.* Gütersloh: Bertelsmann Stiftung.

Wennemann, Adolf. 1997. *Arbeit im Norden. Die Italiener im Rheinland und Westfalen des späten 19. und frühen 20. Jahrhunderts.* Schriften des Instituts für Migrationsforschung und Interkulturelle Studien, vol. 2. Osnabrück: Universitätsverlag Rasch.

Willcox, Walter F., ed. 1929. *International Migrations,* vol. 1, *Statistics.* New York: National Bureau of Economic Research.

Willems, Helmut, Roland Eckert, Stefanie Würtz, and Linda Steinmetz. 1993. *Fremdenfeindliche Gewalt: Einstellungen— Täter—Konflikteskalation.* Opladen: Leske and Budrich.

Wittke, Carl F. 1952. *Refugees of Revolution: The German Forty-Eighters in America.* Philadelphia: University of Pennsylvania Press.

Zucker, Adolf Eduard, ed. 1950. *The Forty-Eighters: Political Refugees of the German Revolution of 1848.* New York: Columbia University Press.

Chapter 2

An Immigration Country of Assimilative Pluralism

Immigrant Reception and Absorption in
American History

Reed Ueda

The *continuous* immigration of the nineteenth and early twentieth
centuries was thus central to the whole American faith. It gave every
old American a standard by which to judge how far he had come and
every new American a realization of how far he might go. It
reminded every American, old and new, that change is the essence of
life, and that American society is a process, not a conclusion.

—John F. Kennedy, 1958

This was America. But America in the uniqueness of its extreme
situation often foreshadowed the destiny of the whole western world
of Europe.

—Oscar Handlin, 1956

Unlike the nation-states of Europe, the United States has historically been a country in which heterogeneity formed the basis
of the state. While the history of European states centered on
consolidating homogeneous ethnic nations, in the United States
the state arose from a democratic-cosmopolitan nation shaped
largely by immigration. Indeed, the United States is usually
classified as the outstanding case of an "immigration country," a
state resting on a transplanted creole population of diverse and
mixed ethnic ancestry.

The United States has qualified as world history's greatest immigration country by virtue of the quantity of immigrants it received and the number of ethnic groups it accommodated. A comparative accounting of U.S. immigration totals reveals the United States' historic role as a uniquely powerful magnet of international population movements. More immigrants went to the United States than to all other great immigration-receiving countries in the world combined. From 1820 to 1930, 38 million people moved to the United States, while 24 million migrated to Canada, Argentina, Brazil, Australia, New Zealand, South Africa, and other areas. From 1945 to the early 1990s, 20 million newcomers flocked to the United States (Bernard 1950, 201; U.S. Immigration and Naturalization Service, 1991, 48–50).

Immigration into the United States reflected an unparalleled historic pattern of ethnic variation. From 1820 to 1945, 16 percent of immigrants to the USA came from Germany, 12 percent from Italy, 12 percent from Ireland, 11 percent from Austria-Hungary, 9 percent from Russia, and 8 percent from Canada, while only 7 percent arrived from England. Smaller fractions of the influx came from Asia, the Middle East, the Caribbean, and Latin America. By contrast, other English-speaking immigration countries drew their settlers almost wholly from other English-speaking nations, and Latin American societies also showed a narrow spectrum of national diversity limited chiefly to Iberian and Italian origins (Bernard 1950, 204, 311)

The Regulation and Reception of Immigrants

Legislation enacted by Congress both shaped and reflected the changing demographic patterns of U.S. immigration. Immigration policy was thus in a constant process of evolution, regulating immigration according not only to the shifting characteristics of immigrants but also to a changing vision of the agenda for national development.

In the century after the American Revolution, immigration policy was guided by the assumptions rooted in ideological republicanism. The U.S. polity embodied in its institutions and operating procedures the principle of political equality. This principle rested on a cosmopolitan faith in the capacity of all men for rational self-rule (Wood 1969, chs. 1–2; Kettner 1974, 208–42). Moreover, the Revolution popularized a new conception of national identity. In their struggle to separate themselves from the English, Americans avowed that they were a new people bred from the frontier and the mingling of several nationalities. The official motto E Pluribus Unum expressed the new government's confidence in the unity that would arise from the diversity of the American people (Mann 1979, 52). In 1776 the pamphleteer Tom Paine declared "Europe and not England, is the parent country of America" (Paine 1776, 84).

A cosmopolitan outlook shaped the federal government's view of the immigrant's place in the new nation. In the Ordinance of 1785, Congress included a guarantee of religious freedom in the Northwest Territories, intending that this protection would act as a stimulus to immigration. At the Constitutional Convention of 1787, James Madison asserted, "That part of America which has encouraged them [the foreigners] most, has advanced most rapidly in population, agriculture, and the arts." In 1792 Alexander Hamilton, secretary of the treasury, noted in his Report on Manufactures that "a perfect equality of religious privileges will probably cause them [immigrants] to flock from Europe to the United States." Hamilton's understudy, Assistant Secretary of State Tench Coxe, publicized the number of religions followed in the United States and the religious freedom held out to all immigrants (Bernard 1980, 488).

During the first century of national government, Congress established the principle of admitting immigrants on the basis of individual qualification. Rights to naturalization were available to all free whites (*U.S. Statutes at large* 1 [1790]:103). The principle of citizenship by territorial birthright, the law of jus soli, ensured that the descendants of immigrants automatically became part of the political community (Schuck and Smith 1985, 52–53).

As a logical corollary to the axiomatic concept of individual citizenship, rights to admission and settlement could not be apportioned according to group origin. Lawmakers consistently refused to support colonization projects aimed at building immigrant communities seeking to retain separate and distinct cultures. For example, in 1817 Congress refused a petition from the Irish Emigrant Society of New York to reserve public lands in Illinois for exclusive settlement by Irish newcomers (Jones 1960, 119). In 1874 Congress received a petition from German Mennonite immigrants for special and exclusive settlement rights. Some federal lawmakers were tempted to give them their own tract of land to keep them from going to Canada. Others took the traditional position that no group had "a separate right to compact themselves as an exclusive community." The controversy ended when three western states offered the Mennonites exemption from militia duty, thus leading most of them to settle in the United States (Higham 1955, 17).

The Republican Party supported an open immigration policy in its presidential and local campaigns. Its 1864 platform, which Abraham Lincoln helped write, announced, "Foreign immigration which in the past has added so much to the wealth, resources, and increase of power to this nation—the asylum of all oppressed nations—should be fostered and encouraged by a liberal and just policy." In 1868 and 1872 the party renewed its promises to use federal power to stimulate immigration (Bernard 1980, 489).

In 1875 a U.S. Supreme Court decision started a tidal change in national immigration policy. In *Henderson v. Mayor of New York*, the court declared unconstitutional all the seaboard states' existing laws controlling the reception of immigrants, having found that they usurped the exclusive power vested in Congress to regulate foreign commerce. The operation of state immigration commissions and port authorities was suddenly declared legally invalid. Soon thereafter, Congress plunged into new legislative activity that produced a series of statutes bringing immigration under direct federal regulation for the first time. The era of decentralized administration of immigration had come to an end (*Reports of the Immigration Commission* 1911, vol. 39).

In the 1870s pressures were building to regulate immigration by using nationality to determine admissions. Labor organizations appealed to Congress to curtail the immigration of Chinese workers, and both the Republican and Democratic parties of the Far Western states agreed that Congress must take regulatory action against the Chinese. Chinese immigration, however, had been approved by the Burlingame Treaty of 1868 (16 Stat. 739:1868): in exchange for trading privileges, it promised China that the free immigration of Chinese to the United States would continue. Thus when Congress passed a bill in 1879 that attempted to restrict Chinese immigration by banning from entry all vessels carrying more than fifteen Chinese passengers, President Rutherford B. Hayes vetoed the bill, claiming that it violated the Burlingame Treaty. A new treaty was negotiated with China in 1880 that permitted the United States to "regulate, limit, or suspend" but "not absolutely prohibit" the migration of Chinese laborers. Finally, in 1882 Congress enacted the Chinese Exclusion Act banning all Chinese laborers and preventing Chinese immigrants from acquiring U.S. citizenship through naturalization (22 Stat. 58:1882).

From 1891 to 1929 Congress built a complex body of law that steadily restricted the categories of immigrants qualified for admission. Its goal was to admit only those who theoretically could be assimilated into the host society. Piece by piece, it enacted measures that set more stringent requirements for immigrants and enlarged the number of excluded categories. In 1891 Congress excluded from admission people likely to become public charges, people with certain contagious diseases, and those convicted of crimes, and polygamists (26 Stat. 1084:1891). The assassination of President William McKinley in 1901 prompted Congress in 1903 to bar anarchists and other subversives from entry (32 Stat. 1213:1903). A 1907 law excluded people with mental defects and those who had committed crimes involving "moral turpitude" (34 Stat. 898:1907).

The restrictions limiting Asian immigration intensified through new legislation. Since the 1870s congressmen and senators from the Far Western states had made the permanent exclusion of Chinese laborers a paramount legislative goal. In 1902 they succeeded in passing a law that indefinitely prohibited the immigration of Chinese workers (32 Stat. 176:1902). About this time, however, new immigrants from Asia, the Japanese, began to arrive in numbers as great as those during the peak years of Chinese immigration. Congress proposed to extend the ban on Chinese immigrants to include the Japanese. Lawmakers also sought to exclude Korean immigrants, whose homeland had been annexed by Japan in 1905. Anti-Asian restrictionism received an unexpected boost in 1907 and 1908 when the so-called Gentleman's Agreement was arranged between Washington and Tokyo (Hing 1993, 207–12): the Japanese government pledged to restrict emigration of Japanese laborers to the United States in exchange for the admission of Japanese-American pupils to San Francisco's public school system.

The Immigration Act of 1917 was a major step toward an omnibus policy of discriminatory restriction based on national origins (39 Stat. 874:1917). It introduced the long-sought literacy test, which its supporters believed would have the practical effect of excluding immigrants from southern and eastern Europe. It established an Asiatic Barred Zone, from which no laborers could come, covering all of India, Afghanistan, and Arabia as well as East Asia and the Pacific. This controversial law was passed over the veto of Woodrow Wilson.

After a slowdown in arrivals, mainly resulting from the international disruptions of World War I, annual immigration rebounded. Restrictionists groped for more drastic devices to stem the flood (Higham 1955, 308). In 1921 legislators introduced a system of discriminatory quotas (42 Stat. 5:1921). Using the Dillingham Immigration Commission findings as evidence, Congress began to devise a ranking system by which groups of particular national origins were preferred over others (Handlin 1957, 77–110). This innovation constituted a turning point in the history of U.S. immigration policy. Henceforth, the number of aliens of any admissible nationality would equal 3 percent of the foreign-born population of that nationality enumerated in the United States census of 1910. These quotas were limited to Europe, the Near East, Africa, Australia, New Zealand, and Siberia. They did not apply to nationalities excluded previously by the Asiatic Barred Zone, Chinese exclusion laws, and the Gentleman's Agreement. They also did not extend to countries in the Western Hemisphere. Finally, the 1921 act installed for the first time an annual ceiling on admissions of 355,000, 200,000 of which were available to immigrants from northern and western Europe and 155,000 going chiefly to those from southern and eastern Europe. This act was passed over yet another veto by Woodrow Wilson.

Spearheaded by delegations from western and southern states, Congress passed the Johnson-Reid Act of 1924 (43 Stat. 153:1924). It barred all Asian immigrants as "aliens ineligible for citizenship" and imposed even smaller quotas on southern and eastern Europe. The annual ceiling on total immigration was set at 2 percent of the foreign-born population in the United States in 1890. The 1890 baseline for quotas favored immigrants from northern and western Europe, since they were more heavily represented in 1890 than in 1910. Resetting the quotas reduced the southern and Eastern European share of annual admissions to only 20 percent.

Restrictionists used the Johnson-Reid Act as a temporary measure before an even more severe restrictive policy was installed in 1929. The annual ceiling for immigration shrank once more, to 150,000. A formal "national origins" plan was invoked in which quotas were allocated to countries on the basis of the proportion of ancestry groups in the U.S. population as enumerated by the 1920 census (Divine 1957, 27–50). Northern and Western European countries received 82 percent of the annual ceiling. Those in southern and eastern Europe received 16 percent, and the rest of the world 2 percent. The national origins system thus met the desired goal of distributing quotas according to a hierarchy of nationalities ranked in grades of assimilability.

In the industrial era, a trans-Atlantic population movement had dominantly shaped the patterns of immigration. Immigration from Asia accounted for only a small percentage of total immigration from 1850 to 1910; mass immigration from Mexico and the Caribbean only began just prior to World War I. The bulk of immigration came from Europe and evolved through two distinct ethnically defined stages. In the first period, from the end of the Napoleonic Wars to the 1870s, immigration from North and West European nations predominated, particularly from Ireland and Germany. Two million Irish immigrants and 1.5 million German immigrants arrived in the three decades before the Civil War (U.S. Immigration and Naturalization Service 1991, 48; Anbinder 1992, 4). They constituted two-thirds of all immigrants who arrived from 1830 to 1860. After 1890 U.S. immigration was fed increasingly by streams originating from southern and eastern Europe. The largest groups among the so-called new immigrants came chiefly from Italy, Austria-Hungary, and Russia (Archdeacon 1983, 121–28). From 1899 to 1924 3.8 million Italians immigrated, 80 percent of them from southern Italy. The peak of Italian immigration to the United States occurred between 1900 and 1914: 3 million Italians arrived during this period. The Slavs formed the second largest group in the new immigration: 3.4 million entered from 1899 to 1924. From 1899 to 1924, among the eastern Slavs, Russians, Ruthenians, and Ukrainians were the most numerous. Among the western Slavs, Poles, Czechs, and Slovakians made up the largest number. And among the southern Slavs, Slovenians and Croatians predominated. Jews from eastern Europe constituted the third major element of the new immigration, accounting for 1.8 million arrivals from 1899 to 1924. Three-quarters of Jewish immigrants from eastern Europe in the United States came from Russian territory. One-quarter came from Romania and the Hapsburg Empire of Austria-Hungary (Galicia, Bukovina, and Hungary). Other groups contributed smaller but substantial numbers. Five hundred thousand Greeks, 500,000 Hungarians, and 300,000 Finns entered the United States from 1899 to 1924. This tremendous flow from southern and eastern Europe was drastically reduced by the imposition of restrictive immigration quotas in 1924.

From the end of the Napoleonic era to the onset of the Great Depression, U.S. immigration developed consistent and distinct demographic features. The annual influx displayed a steady upward trend until the ending of free immigration from Europe but embedded in this trend were short swings of ebb and flow coincident with the economic cycle of growth and recession. The composite demographic pattern stemmed from the predominance of young males, the proletarian character of the labor force, the rising level of return migration, and the growth of immigration from outside northern and western Europe, especially from Asia and southern and eastern Europe (Ueda 1994, 11–15).

In the years between the world wars, lawmakers tended to treat immigration from the Western Hemisphere as a special case apart from all other foreign influxes. Immigration from Canada and Latin America was exempted from nationality quotas and yearly admissions ceilings. Seeking to satisfy agricultural and industrial employers in the Southwest, Congress kept a back door open to cheap labor from Mexico. Congress also introduced a guest-worker program with Mexico in which 4.7 million braceros, or agricultural laborers, were admitted on temporary work contracts from 1943 to 1965 (Fuchs 1990, 120–27).

From World War II to the Vietnam War, the United States gradually overhauled its immigration policy. The dismantling of restrictionist quotas sprang from the new global role for the

United States that had begun with its involvement in World War II. Strengthening the image of the United States as a world democratic leader necessitated recasting immigration policy to reflect the nation's dedication to fair treatment of all nationalities. The postwar reform of admissions and naturalization policy was perhaps the most consequential governmental action furthering the conception of the United States as a world melting pot based on inclusive and unified citizenship. Immigration law came to reflect better than any other body of public policy the view that racial and ethnic distinctions were invalid.

Coupling the historic ideal of immigrant nationhood to the realpolitik of cold war diplomacy, a bill admitting "Displaced Persons," or refugees, from central and eastern Europe passed into law in 1948 (62 Stat. 1009:1948). Later in the decade Congress legislated acts that brought refugees from other places in Europe as well as Asia. Refugees gained admission far in excess of the quota allotments for their home countries, and the United States became the world's leader in refugee admissions. One out of seven immigrants arriving from World War II to 1990—2.5 million immigrants out of a total of 18.6 million—were refugees (Ueda 1994, 50).

The first fault line in the fortress of restriction occurred in 1943, when Congress repealed the Chinese exclusion policy, in force since 1882 (57 Stat. 600:1943). In 1946 Congress permitted the naturalization of immigrants from India and the Philippines and provided a token quota to India (60 Stat. 416:1946). Exclusions according to national origins was no longer an absolute interest of the United States. The 1952 McCarran-Walter Immigration Act reaffirmed the discriminatory quota system but loosened exclusion slightly by setting up small token quotas for immigrants from Asian countries, who had been barred since 1924. All racial prohibitions on naturalization were rescinded. By abolishing Asian exclusion, the McCarran-Walter Act eliminated a principal obstacle to reopening admissions on a worldwide basis.

With the passage of the Hart-Celler immigration act of 1965, the national-origins system of restrictive admissions and exclusion was replaced by a worldwide system of equal per-country visa allotments (79 Stat. 911:1965). Ethnic variation in U.S. immigration increased in unexpected ways. Immigration accelerated from regions in Asia, the Caribbean, Latin America, the

Middle East, and Africa, from which few immigrants had previously come. The yearly arrivals of European immigrants shrank to a small fraction by the 1980s. The Immigration and Naturalization Service reported admissions in 1990 from thirty Asian countries (including the Middle East), seventeen Central and South American countries, thirteen Caribbean countries, and thirteen African countries (U.S. Immigration and Naturalization Service 1991, 52–53).

In the 1970s and 1980s the reform of immigration policy continued to be shaped by congressional and presidential efforts to further U.S. globalism aims during the cold war, but these had the overall effect of expanding opportunities for admission. Special preference categories for family reunification and highly trained personnel enlarged the flow (Fuchs 1990, 279). The United States continued its world leadership in refugee admissions with the passage of the Refugee Act of 1980, which established a permanent mechanism for the admission of refugees (94 Stat. 102:1980). The Immigration Reform and Control Act of 1986 normalized the status of undocumented and illegal immigrants and expanded certain categories of admission (100 Stat. 3349:1986). In 1990 Congress passed another major immigration bill that renewed the worldwide system of regular and refugee admissions (104 Stat. 4978:1990).

The pace of immigration legislation accelerated from 1965, promoting a steady rise in the annual totals of arrivals. The absence of a popular or intellectually potent ideology of restriction combined with the political effectiveness of pro-immigration advocates to produce an admissions policy in which the "values of expansion and diversity prevailed over those of restriction and homogeneity," in the words of legal scholar Peter Schuck (1992, 37–92; see also Loescher and Scanlon 1986). By the mid-1990s, however, faced with rising concerns over the problems of absorbing the mounting foreign population, legislators began to consider new ways to downsize the flow of immigrants.

The Historic Factors Promoting Assimilative Pluralism

The juxtaposition of the enormous pluralism of immigration and widespread ethnic assimilation came to define the social dynamics of the United States in a cardinal way. It resulted from a democratic response to the challenge of multicultural pluralism early in its history that other nations in the old world such as Germany, France, England, and Japan are only facing today. The double position of the United States as the first immigration country in the modern world and the first pluralist democracy made a crucial historical difference in its national development relative to other societies.

After World War II, Germany and other western European societies experimented with ways to become immigration-receiving countries after having built advanced industrial economies in the framework of ethnic nationalism. With strong centralized states, these countries tried a managed approach to immigration. They assumed that government planning and control would handle the needs of immigrants and their impact on the host society. This managed influx was inserted into limited and specific slots in a highly evolved and articulated economy.

In the United States, by contrast, immigration preceded the founding of a national and industrial society. A self-concept emphasizing heterogeneity, not homogeneity, was already expressed in the cosmopolitan citizenship and nationality policies of the early republic. This idea overshadowed the self-image of national homogeneity (Fischer 1989, 595–603, 783–816; McDonald and McDonald 1980, 179–99; Handlin 1963, 149; Handlin and Handlin 1989, 139–40; Crevecoeur 1981, 69–70; Paine 1986, 85; Handlin and Handlin 1992, 85; Fuchs 1990, 16–19).

U.S. immigrants pioneered a creative form of a pluralism that can be described as consensual, voluntary, and democratic. The expansive economy, the process of urban growth, the fluid social structure, and the continuously expanding cultural pluralism produced by mass immigration provided a setting in which ethnic Americans could find niches for self-assertion and acculturation. They utilized the degrees of freedom afforded in the United States to merge with the wider community while maintaining connections with the sphere of ethnic life. Their adaptive strategy was sufficiently flexible and fluid to accommodate successive and superimposed waves of newcomers from changing home societies. The building of relations between immigrants and the host society involved communicating and coexisting with a vast array of different neighbors. Immigrants charted a variety of

vith the concurrent needs of joining the main-
intaining their ethnic lives (Zunz 1982, 91–195;
is. 1–2; Bodnar 1985, chs. 4–6). Further adjust-
community's institutional life and outreach
occurred as second- and third-generation descendants achieved
social mobility, resettled in suburban enclaves, and intermarried
(Lieberson and Waters 1988; Alba 1990). Immigrants exhibited a
dual capacity for repeated self-transformation and reconnection
with their unique heritages. Ethnic relations in the United
States can be compared to a kaleidoscope of old fragments resetting themselves into new and unpredictable patterns, the experiences of each immigrant group being the expressions of the
U.S. pattern of ethnicity, endlessly renewing itself, endlessly
reshaping national life (Fuchs 1990).

The societal problem presented by immigration lay in relating
the parts to the whole, the ethnic fragments to the nation. For
the custodians of the whole—the native legislators, opinion
makers, and educators—the key question was whether national
citizenship could unite the multitudinous subgroups settling in
the country. The nation-building role of citizenship assumed
paramount importance in the quintessential immigration country that was the USA (Marshall 1950; Bendix 1977).

The cosmopolitan and individualistic principles of U.S. con-
stitutionalism possessed a potential for overcoming race and
other accidental collective factors. The republican conception of
U.S. citizenship applied without exception to all individuals of
European origin. Although the Constitution remained ambivalent about race, it provided for the possibility of citizenship of
freed African slaves and their descendants in the northern
states. After the Civil War, the Fourteenth and Fifteenth Amendments expanded the compass of U.S. citizenship to include
emancipated blacks. In the twentieth century, the passage of
laws creating a worldwide system of admissions and naturalization and the antidiscrimination policies springing from the Civil
Rights movement made the United States a country in which
citizenship and nationality were equivalent: all citizens were
members of the nation and all members of the nation were equal
citizens. This development was crucial for the incorporation of
the wave of non-European immigrants arriving after the 1960s
(Wood 1969, 606–15; Horowitz 1992, 12).

The idea of liberal nationalism institutionalized by the American Revolution was the most powerful shaping force of U.S. nationhood (Hobsbawm 1990, 39–40). Its idealistic universalism and individualism expressed through a nationalizing mission of outward movement through an open society toward a greater and higher community evoked a glorious destiny. In the United States, this destiny was promoted in the nineteenth century by expansionists who asserted that Americans conquered by absorption. The self-serving ideology of Manifest Destiny possessed at its core a vision of "elevating" the "misgoverned and oppressed." Those claiming that the United States was "destined to expand by assimilating" backed up their words with the offer of citizenship to foreigners (Mann 1979, 127).

The valorizing of a civic self-identity beyond ethnic origin merged groups with the state and the nation. Immigrant outsiders found this viewpoint compelling and attractive because it supplied a democratic incentive to identify with a centralized political authority that protected the rights of all (Gellner 1983, 2). Liberal nationalism represented the interests of minorities, who came to claim its principles as part of their own essence. The historian Hans Kohn explained: "The American nation was to be a universal nation—not only in the sense that the idea which it pursued was believed to be universal and valid for the whole of mankind but also in the sense that it was a nation composed of many strains. Such a nation, held together by liberty and diversity, had to be firmly integrated around allegiance to the American idea, an idea to which everyone could be assimilated for the very reason that it was a universal idea" (1957, 138).

The principles of liberal nationalism meant that the collective concept of immigrant nationhood would centrally shape the idea of U.S. nationhood. Advocates of liberal nationalism promoted the right of immigrants to assimilate under an inclusive and unifying civic Anglo-Saxonism. Those espousing this integrationist nationalism believed that the transference of both culture and its proprietary possession could effectively occur (Kohn 1957, 150; Solomon 1956, 3–6; Mann 1979, 127–128; Arieli 1964, 87–89).

The republican and liberal framework of the national founding established a generous, protected sphere for the institutions of civil society and individual civil rights. The development of colonies far removed from close imperial supervision favored the power of local community and individuals. The political charters drafted by anti-imperialist rebels limited the reach of government power. The federal and state constitutions gave the sphere of civil society a wide latitude to accommodate a social order of fluidity, pluralism, and voluntary integration. As the historian Yehoshua Arieli pointed out, "In the last analysis, American nationality was based on identification with a 'social system' and its political superstructure" that allowed "the local structure of social life" to be "woven into this texture of nationality" (1964, 77, see also 85–86; see Lipset 1963, chs. 2, 3; Greenfeld 1992, 420–22, 482–83; Handlin and Handlin 1961, 32–48; Glazer 1975, 26–27; Higham 1975, 18–20; Pocock 1975, 523).

The founders' purpose of curtailing centralized power produced a federal structure of government that deeply affected U.S. ethnic relations. Political federalism permitted the unregulated expression of ethnic pluralism. Ethnic groups had opportunities to fashion control over a variety of territorial subcommunities. The political scientist Lawrence H. Fuchs described what he termed the "civic culture" in this sphere: "The civic culture, with its principles of separation of church and state and the right of free speech and assembly, facilitated and protected the expression of ancestral cultural values and sensibilities and, in so doing, sanctioned the system of voluntary pluralism by which ethnic groups could mobilize their economic and political interests" (1990, 23). The pursuit of group interests and recognition could occur through local and regional impulses toward power. The decentralization of ethnic politics provided sufficient openings for the various assertions of communal self-determination. It was a safety valve for ethnic rivalries and tensions that diverted group conflicts from dominating national governance (Horowitz 1992, 23–25; Glazer 1983, 274–92).

The constitutions of the Revolutionary era did not give political status to ethnic groups or collective cultures. Federal and state constitutions only covered citizens; the U.S. polity merely tolerated the development of ethnic subcultures and institutions based on a variety of religions. Government policy toward ethnic subcultures therefore closely paralleled the principle of religious disestablishment. State officials did not sponsor the establishment of religious institutions, ethnic newspapers, language schools, and ethnic mutual aid societies. Government's avoidance of involvement in communal life further encouraged immigrants to initiate and take responsibility for communal institutional affairs (Rahe 1994, 3:214–16; Jones 1960, 123; Higham 1955, 17; Correll 1946, 183–216).

Ethnic relations for immigrant groups in the United States developed along a course divergent from that in France and opposite from that in Germany. In the area between nationhood and ethnic groups established by a pluralist democracy, immigrants and their descendants possessed the right to assimilate *and* the right to preserve ethnic qualities. It was possible to become an ethnic U.S. citizen—to be Italian American or Japanese American—rather than to become French through cultural assimilation or to be German through ethnic descent. As Liah Greenfeld put the matter, "Dual identity thus remained typical," and as national integration proceeded, persons with parochial loyalties "were replaced by hyphenated Americans" (Greenfeld 1992, 482; see Horowitz 1992, 12–13; Brubaker 1992, 97–98).

Permeable boundaries between a multiplicity of immigrant groups came to define the character of ethnic relations. Because immigrants exercised extensive self-determination and self-maintenance in their cultural and social existence, ethnic identity and national identity coexisted in a kind of deregulated balance. A pluralism based on consent—the individual's elective option to change or preserve traditions and to create new attachments for collective identity—made possible a pluralism that was assimilative. Immigrant ethnic groups never became isolated, and national life depended on openness toward them. Even the Anglo-Saxon core became porous; the charter group could not preserve a totally separate sphere of existence. As a consequence of these transactional processes, immigrant groupings evolved from an initial phase of differentiation to accommodation, integration, and finally consolidation in the patterns of national life.

The effectiveness of its assimilative ethnic pluralism set the United States apart from traditional plural societies such as India, Austria-Hungary, the Russian Empire, and the Ottoman Empire. Immigration was the principal shaping force of this absorptive factor. Immigration ensured that the patterns of pluralism would not become preformed and predetermined. Rather than becoming petrified cultural roots, they unfolded progressively as living and creative forms capable of absorbing new traditions. Impinging recurrently on the rebuilding of a society and its institutions, the periodic cycles of immigration constituted a dynamic force that endowed the United States with an undelimited capacity for social transformation, making it "a permanently unfinished country." Because the ever-changing patterns of pluralism exercised an assimilative power, the United States, the immigration country par excellence, sustained itself as a unified democracy in the twentieth century (Higham 1975, 18–20; Glazer 1975, 26–27; Franklin, Pettigrew, and Mack 1971, 34).

These open patterns of cultural and social pluralism did not exist full-blown and continuously through the span of national history. They were historically constructed, evolving gradually in a matrix of political and civic conditions that grew more racially inclusive over time.

German Immigrants as a Case Study in Assimilative Pluralism

The involvement of immigrant groups in the patterns of assimilative pluralism followed a rough sequence corresponding to time of arrival. The group life of immigrants from northern and western Europe who composed the earliest influx was incorporated within the dynamics of an assimilative pluralism in the earliest and most developed way. The history of the ethnic community arising out of German immigration provides a revealing illustration of this process.

More immigrants to the United States came from Germany than from any other country. During the eighteenth century at least 65,000 and perhaps as many as 100,000 immigrants arrived, chiefly from the Rhenish Palatinate (Conzen 1980, 407). The large majority were Protestant sectarians. This flow to North America was newer and smaller than the historic and massive migration of Catholic Germans eastward into Hapsburg lands and Russia. In the 1830s, however, trans-Atlantic migration for the first time surpassed the continental flow to the east (Bade 1995, 400). The United States became the principal destination. From 1820 to 1990 7 million immigrants arrived from Germany, constituting 15 percent of the total of all immigrants to the United States. Protestants made up over half of all German immigrants, while Catholics composed a third, and Jews the remainder (Conzen 1980, 417).

The period from 1840 to 1890 constituted the high tide of German immigration. Over these five decades, 4.5 million German immigrants arrived (U.S. Immigration and Naturalization Service 1990, table 2). In the 1880s, the peak historical decade of immigration from Germany, 1.4 million German newcomers came to the United States.

As the largest immigrant ethnic population in the era of the agricultural and industrial revolutions, German Americans shaped the growth of the nineteenth-century economy, perhaps more broadly than any other immigrant group. They played a central role in the expansion of craftsmanship and the commercialization of family farming. In 1870 37 percent of employed German immigrants held skilled occupations, 27 percent were farmers, 23 percent worked in professional and service fields, and 13 percent in trade and transportation (Conzen 1980, 413). German immigrants predominated in these fields, particularly in the upper Mississippi and Ohio River valleys, where half of all German-born people in the United States lived (Sowell 1996, 72).

Germans made up the largest ethnic element among all U.S. farmers. In 1870 one out of three foreign-born farmers was a German immigrant (Conzen 1980, 415). By 1900 they owned 11 percent of all U.S. farms. In 1880 German farmers in eastern Texas outproduced other Texan farmers (Sowell 1996, 72). In the 1930s Germans owned most of the sugar beet farms in Colorado, Montana, and Wyoming.

The German presence in industry and artisanship was equally important. German immigrants were numerous in the ranks of skilled urban workingmen. In nineteenth-century Milwaukee, St. Louis, New York City, Detroit, and Boston, Germans made up a large share of the so-called labor aristocracy. German skilled workers specialized in cabinetmaking, tailoring, and cigar making and dominated many food-preparation fields, such as butchering, baking, brewing, and distilling.

Among first- and second-generation Germans there were also many educators, church leaders, engineers, academics, physicians, lawyers, and other professionals. German Americans diversified the occupational spectrum and galvanized the patterns of social mobility in immigrant America.

Successful economic adaptation was coupled with a vigorous ethnic communal life. German farmers and artisans lived in enclaves that reflected the particular subregions of Germany from which they sprang. Local communal networks formed the basis of many small-scale enterprises. The historian Olivier Zunz found in his study of industrializing Detroit among "skilled and unskilled workers, the Germans were the most likely to be employed within their own community": "They occupied every variety of skilled position, many working for large industrial concerns but as many being independent craftsmen, often employing a few men of their own. The Bureau of Labor's factory inspection reports are filled with these small east-side shops run by Germans—the small hat factory with five workers, or the local newspaper with a work force of four, or the small bookbindery, or the jewelry or fabric store, or the small cigar factory" (1982, 224.) In the words of historian Kathleen Neils Conzen, the urban concentrations of Germans created "virtually self-sufficient neighborhood communities based on shared activities, voluntary associations, and formal institutions" (1980, 415). A report to the U.S. Office of Education described the German communities of South Dakota: "Some counties—Hutchinson, for example—are largely peopled by German stock. In this county and in Hanson County the German-Russian Mennonites still live the quaint community life brought with them from Russia. German, not English, is the language of the villages, although in most of the schools English is the language of instruction" (Thompson 1920, 147). Rural midwestern communities like Schleswig, Iowa, comprised nearly homogeneous clusterings of Germans who had emigrated from particular localities. The ethnic community and its families served as the social basis for the aggregate development of farmlands.

Whether rural or urban, the residential clusters of Germans exhibited a vigorous spirit of ethnocultural maintenance. In this respect, German-American communities epitomized the pattern of democratic consensual pluralism in the United States. They took advantage of the freedom offered by the large sphere of civil society to cultivate their own civic and cultural institutions. Germans established an innumerable variety of associational clubs (Conzen 1976, ch. 6), including volunteer fire and militia companies, music societies, mutual-benefit lodges, recreational clubs, and dramatic societies. A national roster compiled in 1915 listed four cities with more than two hundred German-American clubs (416–17). Germans established churches wherever they settled. German Catholics used the church as a base for parochial schools that taught religious values and the German language. The Central Verein represented German Catholics nationally in the politics and management of social reform (Gleason 1968). On the basis of these associational patterns, the political scientist Lawrence H. Fuchs argued, "German immigrants and their children, more than any other group, provided a large-scale early example of the process of ethnic-Americanization, in which ancestral loyalties (religious, linguistic, and cultural) are changed (and in some ways strengthened) to American circumstances even as immigrants and their children embrace American political ideals and participate in American political institutions" (1990, 20).

The historian Frederick C. Luebke pointed out that "the German language became the chief agent for the perpetuation of immigrant cultural forms" (1990, 171). This was especially true after the 1890s, when the flow of immigrants who reinforced the ancestral culture underwent sharp decline. Germans continued to use German as the chief public language of their enclaves even into the twentieth century. It was the spoken language on many streets in Cincinnati, St. Louis, and Milwaukee. German Americans created and supported the largest foreign language press in the country. A survey by a Chicago sociologist, Robert E. Park, showed that in 1884 out of 794 foreign-language newspapers, 621 were in German (Tsuchida 1989, 96). In 1892 the number of German-language newspapers reached an all-time high of 794.

The vibrancy of German-American ethnicity perhaps reached a pinnacle around the turn of the century, but the unexpected crises of World War I and cultural change from intergenerational succession then led to progressive assimilation. The anti-German atmosphere generated by the war placed intense public pressure on German Americans to renounce their cultural and linguistic traditions. The attack on the maintenance of the German language produced a dramatic erosion of the linguistic basis of German institutions and communities. Many educational institutions in the enclave communities no longer afforded instruction of German or in German. From the peak of 794 in 1892, the number of German language newspapers in the country had shrunk to 276 by 1920 (Tsuchida 1989, 96).

As the number of German newspapers dwindled to 81 in 1940 and to 33 by 1960, they served as a barometer of the cultural assimilation of German Americans. The ebbing tide of mass migration, the restriction of immigration after the 1920s, the process of upward social mobility, the absorption into secular middle-class culture, the impact of two world wars that forced German Americans to "disidentify" with the homeland, the residential mobility that depleted enclaves, and, above all, the rising rate of intermarriage (67 percent of Americans in 1979 with a German ancestor claimed multiple ancestry) turned one of the most vigorous ethnic subcultures in the United States into a melting fragment increasingly indistinguishable in the mainstream (U.S. Bureau of the Census 1982, 7). From this perspective, the history of the Germans in the United States can be regarded as the classic case of an immigrant group being transformed under the conditions existing in a pluralistic democracy. Responding to the liberalizing forces of assimilative pluralism, German Americans demonstrated how it was possible to develop an extraordinary communal ethnicity for a sustained period and also how the inescapable changes brought by social mobility and acculturation prevented this ethnicity from being maintained indefinitely.

The generations of German Americans showed how an immigrant ethnic group could leave their imprint on national life and national culture. Old universals disintegrated as they encountered new particularisms introduced through the transplantation of German culture. Over the course of two or three generations, however, the latter were reformatted into new inclusive totalities that stood for wider patterns. The economist Thomas Sowell explained this general process by describing how it worked to nationalize elements of German American subculture:

> Over the years, Germans have made major contributions to many aspects of American society. In addition to the contributions of broad masses of German people in agriculture and industry, and of German food, customs, and attitudes toward recreation, numerous individuals of German ancestry made historic contributions in various

fields ... . Firms established by individuals of German ancestry have been among the leaders in many American industries, including optics (Bausch and Lomb), wood products (Weyerhauser), automobiles (Chrysler), pianos (Steinway, Schnabel), organs (Wurlitzer), candy (Hershey), prepared food (Heinz), language instruction (Berlitz), and innumerable beer companies, including Anheuser-Busch, Miller, Coors, Pabst, Schlitz, and Blatz. Germans are no longer a distinctive group in America because they have become so much a part of American society and that society has absorbed so many German cultural features, from kindergartens to Christmas trees to coleslaw. With the passing generations, as the German language slowly faded away, many of the cultural features of German-American life became features of American life in general. (Sowell 1996, 82; see Sowell 1981, 58).

The history of German Americans exemplified the permeability of the national culture to introduced ethnic elements and the way it produced a self-recreating national culture. In the 1880s the frankfurter was seen as an ethnic food novelty in areas with large German settlements. A century later, in the 1980s, with the melting away of German ethnic communities, it was seen as the symbol of all-American food to be contrasted with "real" ethnic food. At a 1989 Fourth of July celebration in the multiracial suburb of Monterey Park, California, a Chinese girl hawked hot dogs, shouting, "Get your hot dogs here, they're so American," while a rival male vendor replied, "No, hot dogs are an American cliché. Expand your cultural experiences. Eat an egg roll" (Horton 1992, 240). The subtle reshaping of the national culture by German Americans—or for that matter, by any other immigrant population whose culture has passed into wider circles beyond the ethnic enclave—could easily escape notice, as this amusing anecdote illustrates. Perhaps this trivial incident was actually a significant expression of the efficacy of the historic patterns of assimilative pluralism in the United States (Brown and Bass 1985, 449; Horton 1992, 240).

References

Alba, Richard D. 1990. *Ethnic Identity: The Transformation of White America*. New Haven: Yale University Press.

Anbinder, Tyler. 1992. *Nativism and Slavery: The Northern Know Nothings and the Politics of the 1850s*. New York: Oxford University Press.

Archdeacon, Thomas. 1983. *Becoming American: An Ethnic History*. New York: Free Press.

Arieli, Yehoshua. 1964. *Individualism and Nationalism in American Ideology*. Cambridge: Harvard University Press.

Bade, Klaus J. 1995. "Migration Past and Present—The German Experience." In *People in Transit: German Migrations in Comparative Perspective, 1820–1930*, ed. Dirk Horder and Jorg Nagler. Cambridge: Cambridge University Press.

Bendix, Reinhard. 1977. *Nation-Building and Citizenship*. Berkeley: University of California Press.

Bernard, William S. 1980. "Immigration: History of U.S. Policy." In *Harvard Encyclopedia of American Ethnic Groups*, ed. Stephan Thernstrom. Cambridge: Harvard University Press.

_____. 1950. *American Immigration Policy*. New York: Harper and Brothers.

Bodnar, John. 1985. *The Transplanted: A History of Immigrants in Urban America*. Bloomington: Indiana University Press.

Brown, Richard, and Herbert Bass. 1985. *One Flag, One Land*. Morristown, N.J.: Silver, Burdett.

Brubaker, Rogers. 1992. *Citizenship and Nationhood in France and Germany*. Cambridge: Harvard University Press.

Cohen, Lizabeth. 1990. *Making a New Deal: Industrial Workers in Chicago, 1919–1939*. Cambridge: Cambridge University Press.

Conzen, Kathleen Neils. 1980. "Germans." In *Harvard Encyclopedia of American Ethnic Groups*, ed. Stephan Thernstrom. Cambridge: Harvard University Press.

_____. 1976. *Immigrant Milwaukee, 1836–1860: Accommodation and Community in a Frontier City*. Cambridge: Harvard University Press.

Correll, Ernest, ed. 1946. "The Congressional Debates on the Mennonite Immigration from Russia, 1873–1874." *Mennonite Quarterly Review* 20, no. 2: 178–221.

Crevecoeur, J. Hector St. John de. 1981. *Letters from an American Farmer*. 1782. Reprint. New York: Viking Penguin.

Divine, Robert. 1957. *American Immigration Policy, 1924–1952*. New Haven: Yale University Press.

Fischer, David H. 1989. *Albion's Seed: Four British Folkways in America*. New York: Oxford University Press.

Franklin, John Hope, Thomas F. Pettigrew, and Raymond W. Mack. 1971. *Ethnicity in American Life*. New York: Anti-Defamation League of B'nai B'rith.

Fuchs, Lawrence H. 1990. *The American Kaleidoscope: Race, Ethnicity, and the Civic Culture*. Hanover, N.H.: University Press of New England/Wesleyan.

Gellner, Ernest. 1983. *Nations and Nationalism*. Oxford, England: Blackwell.

Glazer, Nathan. 1983. *Ethnic Dilemmas, 1964–1982*. Cambridge: Harvard University Press.

_____. 1975. *Affirmative Discrimination: Ethnic Inequality and Public Policy*. New York: Basic.

Gleason, Philip. 1968. *The Conservative Reformers: German-American Catholics and the Social Order*. Notre Dame: University of Notre Dame Press.

Greenfeld, Liah. 1992. *Nationalism: Five Roads to Modernity*. Cambridge: Harvard University Press.

Handlin, Oscar. 1982. "Education and the European Immigrant, 1820–1920." In *American Education and the European Immigrant, 1840–1940*, ed. Bernard J. Weiss. Urbana: University of Illinois Press.

_____. 1963. *The Americans: A New History of the People of the United States*. Boston: Little, Brown.

_____. 1957. *Race and Nationality in American Life*. Boston: Little, Brown.

Handlin, Oscar, and Mary Handlin. 1961. *The Dimensions of Liberty*. Cambridge: Harvard University Press.

Handlin, Oscar, and Lilian Handlin. 1992. *Liberty in Peril, 1850–1920*. New York: HarperCollins.

_____. 1989. *Liberty in Expansion, 1760–1850*. New York: Harper and Row.

Higham, John. 1975. *Send These to Me: Jews and Other Immigrants in Urban America*. New York: Atheneum.

_____. 1970. "The Reorientation of American Culture in the 1890's." In *Writing American History: Essays on Modern Scholarship*. Bloomington: Indiana University Press.

_____. 1955. *Strangers in the Land: Patterns of American Nativism, 1860–1925*. New Brunswick: Rutgers University Press.

Hing, Bill Ong. 1993. *Making and Remaking Asian America through Immigration Policy, 1850–1990*. Stanford: Stanford University Press.

Hobsbawm, E. J. 1990. *Nations and Nationalism since 1780: Programme, Myth, Reality*. Cambridge: Cambridge University Press.

Horowitz, Donald L. 1992. "Immigration and Group Relations." In *Immigration and Group Relations in France and America*, ed. Donald L. Horowitz and Gerard Noiriel. New York: New York University Press.

Horton, John. 1992. "The Politics of Diversity in Monterey Park, California." In *Structuring Diversity: Ethnographic Perspectives on the New Immigration*, ed. Louise Lamphere. Chicago: University of Chicago Press.

Jones, Maldwyn Allen. 1960. *American Immigration*. Chicago: University of Chicago Press.

Kennedy, John F. 1964. *A Nation of Immigrants*. Rev. ed. New York: Harper and Row.

Kettner, James H. 1974. "The Development of American Citizenship in the Revolutionary Era: The Idea of Volitional Allegiance." *American Journal of Legal History* 18: 208–42.

Kohn, Hans. 1957. *American Nationalism: An Interpretive Essay*. New York: Macmillan.

Lieberson, Stanley, and Mary C. Waters. 1988. *From Many Strands: Ethnic and Racial Groups in Contemporary America*. New York: Russell Sage.

Lipset, Seymour Martin. 1963. *The First New Nation*. New York: Basic.

Loescher, Gil, and John Scanlan. 1986. *Calculated Kindness: Refugees and America's Half-Open Door, 1945 to the Present*. New York: Free Press.

Luebke, Frederick C. 1990. *Germans in the New World: Essays in the History of Immigration*. Urbana: University of Illinois Press.

McDonald, Forrest, and Ellen S. McDonald. 1980. "The Ethnic Origins of the American People, 1790." *William and Mary Quarterly Review*, 3d ser., 37, no. 2: 179–99.

Mann, Arthur. 1979. *The One and the Many: Reflections on the American Identity*. Chicago: University of Chicago Press.

Marshall, T. H. 1950. *Citizenship and Social Class and Other Essays*. Cambridge: Cambridge University Press.

Paine, Thomas. 1986. *Common Sense*. 1776. Reprint. New York: Penguin.

Pocock, J. G. A. 1975. *The Machiavellian Moment: Florentine Political Thought and the Atlantic Republican Tradition*. Princeton: Princeton University Press.

Rahe, Paul A. 1994. *Republics Ancient and Modern*. Vol. 3. Chapel Hill: University of North Carolina Press.

Reports of the Immigration Commission. 1911. 42 vols. Washington, D.C.: U.S. Government Printing Office.

Schuck, Peter H. 1992. "The Politics of Rapid Legal Change: Immigration Policy in the 1980s." *Studies in American Political Development* 6 (spring 1992): 37–92.

Schuck, Peter H., and Rogers M. Smith. 1985. *Citizenship Without Consent: Illegal Aliens in the American Polity*. New Haven: Yale University Press.

Solomon, Barbara Miller. 1956. *Ancestors and Immigrants: A Changing New England Tradition*. Cambridge: Harvard University Press.

Sowell, Thomas. 1996. *Migrations and Cultures: A World View*. New York: Basic.

_____. 1981. *Ethnic America: A History*. New York: Basic.

Thompson, Frank V. 1920. *Schooling of the Immigrant*. New York: Harper and Brothers.

Tsuchida, Motoko. 1989. "Making of the Americans: Journalism in the Politically Organized Society." The Journal of American and Canadian Studies (autumn): 71–113.

Ueda, Reed. 1994. *Postwar Immigrant America: A Social History*. New York: St. Martin's.

U.S. Bureau of the Census. 1982. *Current Population Reports*. Series P-23, no. 116, *Ancestry and Language in the United States: November 1979*. Washington, D.C.: U.S. Government Printing Office.

U.S. Immigration and Naturalization Service. 1991. *Statistical Yearbook*. Washington, D.C.: U.S. Government Printing Office.

_____. 1990. *Statistical Yearbook*. Washington, D.C.: U.S. Government Printing Office.

Wood, Gordon S. 1969. *The Creation of the American Republic, 1776–1787*. Chapel Hill: University of North Carolina Press.

Zunz, Olivier. 1982. *The Changing Face of Inequality: Urbanization, Industrial Development, and Immigrants in Detroit, 1880–1920*. Chicago: University of Chicago Press.

Chapter 3

Changing Patterns of Immigration to Germany, 1945–1995

Ethnic Origins, Demographic Structure, Future Prospects

Rainer Münz and *Ralf Ulrich*

Introduction

"Germany is not a country of immigration." For decades this has been the official view of the German government in defining its position on international migration and the integration of foreigners.[1] This official stand also reflects the view of many Germans. In line with the German Constitution and the law on citizenship, a majority of them see their country as an ethnically defined nation-state. Germany's self-definition as a nonimmigrant society is thus to be understood as a normative statement: "Germany should not be a country of immigration today and must not become one in the future."

In the past fifty years, however, West Germany has been one of the countries receiving the highest number of immigrants in the world. In 1950 some 8 million of the 50 million inhabitants of the Federal Republic of Germany (FRG) were postwar refugees and expellees *(Vertriebene)*.[2] Since then, West Germany's population has increased by 16 million (to 66 million in

---

Notes for this chapter begin on page 110.

1994). Some 80 percent of this increase can be explained by net migration gains (12.9 million between 1950 and 1994).

In the German Democratic Republic in 1950 3.6 out of 18.4 million GDR citizens were postwar refugees and expellees. In the ensuing years, East Germany was confronted with periods of extremely high emigration, and its regime finally collapsed as a result of mass emigration in 1989–90. During this period (1950–94), despite an excess of births over deaths, East Germany's population declined by 2.9 million, numbering 15.5 million in 1994. This was the result of the substantial losses stemming from migration. Between 1950 and 1994 East Germany lost 4.9 million people to West Germany alone.

Since the end of World War II, more than 20 million people have immigrated to the western part of Germany: expellees, ethnic Germans from Central and Eastern Europe *(Aussiedler)*, Germans from the GDR *(Übersiedler)*, labor migrants (so-called guest workers), asylum seekers, and refugees. This figure only includes people who have stayed in the Federal Republic of Germany for extended periods of time. Since 1950 the population of Germany as a whole (East and West) has increased by 13.1 million, bringing its total population to 81.5 million in 1994. Two-thirds of this increase is due to the positive net migration balance of more than 8 million between 1950 and 1994, not including migration between East and West Germany (see table 3.1).

Table 3.1 Population of Germany, 1950–1994 (in millions)

Year[1]	West Germany	East Germany	Germany
1950	50.0	18.4	68.4
1960	55.4	17.2	72.6
1970	60.6	17.1	77.7
1980	61.5	16.7	78.2
1990	63.7	16.1	79.4
1994	66.0	15.5	81.5
total change	+16.0	–2.9	13.1
net migration balance 1950–1994	+12.9	4.9[2]	+8.0

1. As of 31 December.
2. Net migration balance between East and West Germany only.

Source: Data from the Statistisches Bundesamt; Dorbritz and Gärtner 1995; Schulz 1994; Wendt 1994; the authors' calculations.

One of the peculiarities of immigration to Germany is the large number of immigrants with German citizenship or at least a legal claim to it. Since 1945 more than 50 percent of the immigrants to West Germany have been either ethnic Germans or Germans by law. Half of them came to Germany (within its present borders) at the end of World War II or shortly thereafter, part of the wave of refugees and expellees from eastern parts of the former Reich, as well as from Czechoslovakia, Poland, Hungary, and Yugoslavia.

Six phases of postwar immigration to Germany can be distinguished (see table 3.2; see also Martin 1991; Münz and Ulrich 1993; Rudolph 1994; Seifert 1995). The first phase was dominated by the immigration of Germans: expellees, citizens of the GDR, other ethnic Germans. Recruitment of foreign labor began in the mid-1950s, initiating the second phase. But foreign labor was of no major importance until 1960–61, when the migration from the GDR to the FRG came to a sudden halt after the construction of the Berlin Wall. At this point, the third phase, the German authorities began to organize labor recruitment on a large scale; it was later stopped in order to reduce the number of foreigners in the FRG. This goal was not achieved, but the attempt led to a consolidation of the guest-worker population and later to a new moderate growth in West Germany's foreign population by way of family reunion and a rapidly increasing number of children born to foreigners in Germany (fourth phase). But only in the late 1980s and early 1990s (fifth phase) did the immigration of ethnic Germans and foreigners reach new peak levels. This was due not only to a change in the push and pull factors but also to the dismantling of the Iron Curtain and administrative barriers that, before 1989–90, had rendered regular travel and emigration almost impossible for citizens of Central and East European countries and the USSR. With the introduction of new restrictive measures aiming to limit the immigration of both ethnic Germans and asylum seekers, Germany has now entered the sixth phase of its postwar migration history.

In the past, some push and pull factors existed for GDR citizens, ethnic Germans, and foreigners alike. However, the dynamics of immigration and emigration have to be explained separately for each of the different groups. Legal conditions and individual perspectives were not the same. GDR citizens and ethnic Germans coming to West Germany from Eastern Europe and Central Asia hardly ever thought of returning some day to their countries of origin, whereas some of the foreign laborers and asylum seekers did. The chances of being successfully integrated into Germany's economic and social life also differed among these groups.

Table 3.2 Phases in the History of German Migration, 1945–1995

1945 to 1949	Mainly immigration of ethnic German refugees and expellees *(Vertriebene)* and remigration of non-German forced labor, prisoners of war, and survivors of the concentration camps of Nazi Germany.
1949 to 1961	First peak of migration between East and West Germany *(Übersiedler)*.
1961 to 1973	Active recruitment of foreign labor by the FRG (guest workers); rapid growth of foreign population.
1973 to 1988–89	Recruitment stop; failed attempts to reduce the number of foreigners living in the FRG; consolidation and further growth of the foreign population in West Germany by way of family reunion; recruitment of foreign labor by the GDR.
1988 to 1991	Immigration of ethnic Germans *(Aussiedler)*, asylum seekers, refugees, new labor migrants; second peak of migration between East and West Germany.
since 1992	Introduction of new restrictions against the immigration of *Aussiedler* and asylum seekers

Migration of Ethnic Germans and German Citizens

Expellees and Other Ethnic German Immigrants

The first phase of immigration at the end of World War II and immediately thereafter consisted mainly of refugees and expellees from the Eastern parts of the German Reich as well as from Poland, Czechoslovakia, Hungary, and Yugoslavia. The census of 10 October 1946, registered 5.9 million refugees and expellees in the British and U.S. zones and 3.6 million in the Soviet zone (the French military government in Germany did not allow the resettlement of expellees in the French zone). The census of 13 March 1950, counted 7.9 million refugees and expellees living in West Germany (FRG). By the beginning of the 1950s approximately 12 million ethnic Germans from the former eastern parts of the Reich and from East Central Europe had emigrated to the FRG, the GDR, and Austria (Benz 1985; Stanek 1985). When comparing the number and share of these immigrants in the GDR (3.6 million, i.e., 20 percent of total population) and the FRG (7.9 million, or 16 percent of the total population), we see that the demographic impact was somewhat larger in the east. To a certain extent, the fact that this migration was a result of expulsion, forced resettlement, and ethnic cleansing might explain the greater degree to which these migrants were accepted within East and West German society at that time (Frantzioch 1987).

From 1950 to 1987 immigration of ethnic Germans from Eastern Europe continued on a lesser scale (see figure 3.1). During this period, 1.4 million newly arriving *Aussiedler* were registered in the FRG. The immigration of ethnic Germans, based on bilateral agreements between the West German and the Polish, Romanian, and Soviet governments, stemmed from individual decisions and no longer from ethnic cleansing. This is the main reason for an analytical distinction between *Vertriebene* of the period from 1945 to 1949 and other *Aussiedler* who have come since the 1950s. It is true that ethnic Germans were discriminated against in Poland, Romania, and the former Soviet Union even after 1950; however, individuals requesting emigration to West Germany (and, in rarer cases, to the GDR) calculated the costs and benefits of such a move. Over the last decades, however, German public and political circles have often tended to interpret the decisions of ethnic Germans to emigrate as a response to political and social discrimination and an adherence to the concept of Germanhood and to the political system of (West) Germany (Bethlehem 1982; Delfs 1993; Ronge 1993). The migration of ethnic Germans was and is hardly ever seen as a purely economic decision.

From the beginning of the 1950s the socialist countries restricted the mobility of ethnic Germans as much as that of members of other ethnic groups. After organized expulsion and forced resettlement came to an end, the legal emigration of ethnic Germans was limited to only a few cases of family reunion: 47,000 in 1950 and a mere 5,000 in 1952. During the following

Figure 3.1 Immigration of Ethnic Germans to the FRG by Country of Origin, 1950–1996 (in thousands)

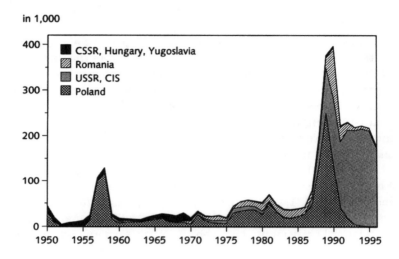

Source: Information from Bundesverwaltungsamt, Bundesministerium des Inneren.

thirty-five years (1953–87), an average number of 37,000 *Aussiedler* a year arrived in Germany. Annual fluctuations in the numbers of *Aussiedler* mostly can be related to periods of internal political liberalization (Poland in the second half of the 1950s, Czechoslovakia in 1967–68, the USSR after 1986), but Poland and Romania in particular used concessions concerning the emigration of ethnic Germans in order to negotiate economic and financial aid with the FRG. With Romania, the West German government even agreed to pay a certain amount of compensation per ethnic German allowed to emigrate. Similar negotiations took place between the East and West German governments.

Between 1950 and 1987 62 percent of all ethnic German immigrants came from Poland (848,000), and 15 percent came from Romania (206,000). In spite of the fact that the Soviet Union also had a large German minority living within its borders, only 110,000 of them (8 percent of all *Aussiedler*) were able to emigrate during this period (see figure 3.1). Even though some internal migration took place, the larger share of German minorities remained within their traditional areas of settlement (Upper Silesia, Transylvania, Banat) or in the regions to which they had been forcefully relocated during or shortly after World War II (e.g., Siberia, Kazakhstan, Kyrgyzstan).

With the fall of the Iron Curtain and the lifting of administrative restrictions on travel in the late 1980s, the migration barriers for ethnic Germans vanished, and the number of ethnic German immigrants rose sharply. In 1988 203,000 ethnic Germans came to the FRG, almost three times the number in the previous year. In 1990 the immigration of ethnic Germans reached its peak: 397,000 *Aussiedler* came to Germany that year. From 1988 to 1994 a total of 1.9 million ethnic Germans immigrated. And the hierarchy of countries of origin had changed: in recent years the Soviet Union and its successor states (CIS) are the main source of ethnic German immigrants (1,057,000, or 57 percent), followed by Poland (590,000, or 32 percent), and Romania (208,000, or 11 percent; see figure 3.1).

For decades, members of German minorities living in socialist countries were not able to emigrate freely, but their immigration was not restricted by Germany. They had the possibility of asking for naturalization while temporarily staying in Germany, for example, while visiting relatives or even after entering illegally. As a rule, they were able to stay on in Germany and given immediate access to German citizenship. In the late 1980s, however, the German government reacted to the liberalization of migration barriers in the countries of origin and the subsequent rise in the number of ethnic German immigrants, and in 1990 German parliament passed a law regulating (and in fact restricting) the immigration of ethnic Germans (Aussiedleraufnahmegesetz). Thus since July 1990 potential immigrants as a rule must apply for admission to Germany in the countries they live in. Applicants must complete a questionnaire of over fifty pages in order to prove their ethnic origins. And the decision is no longer made unbureaucratically and quickly, which has led to a backlog of undecided cases (520,000 in 1995). By 1991 the new regulations had already had the intended effect: the number of ethnic German immigrants accepted in Germany had fallen to 221,000.

In 1992 a special law defining this immigration as a late consequence of World War II (Kriegsfolgenbereinigungsgesetz) fixed a yearly quota of ethnic Germans allowed to enter the country. This quota was set along the lines of the average number of these immigrants in 1991–92: 220,000. In 1994 222,000 ethnic Germans came to Germany. The new law also restricted the right to immigrate to ethnic Germans living on the territory of the former Soviet Union. Other ethnic Germans living in Central and Eastern Europe can only apply after proving that they suffer personally from ethnic discrimination or pressure to emigrate. Finally the law sets an end to future ethnic German immigration: After the year 2010 ethnic Germans born after December 1992 will no longer be entitled to ask independently for admission to Germany. The door, however, will still be left open to immigration on the grounds of family reunion.

Between 1950 and 1994 a total of about 3.2 million ethnic Germans immigrated to Germany. Most of them came from Poland (1.4 million) and the Soviet Union and its successor states (1.4 million). The potential for further immigration by members of this group is difficult to define. The successor states of former Yugoslavia, the Czech Republic, and Slovakia have very few ethnic Germans left. In Romania the large wave of emigration from 1989 to 1992, encouraged by Germany itself, reduced the ethnic German minority to a group of probably not more than 90,000 individuals in 1995, most of them being too old or unwilling to leave their area of settlement. In Poland the number of people considering themselves to be ethnic Germans is estimated at 500,000 to 800,000. Many of them have successfully applied for German citizenship but not yet left the country. An estimated 200,000 to 250,000 people are now holding both German and Polish citizenship, representing a considerable migration potential beyond the new restrictions set up by the law dealing with late consequences of World War II (Kriegsfolgenbereinigungsgesetz).[3]

For a number of reasons, population censuses in Central and Eastern Europe and the successor states of the Soviet Union (CIS and the Baltics) do not give a clear picture of the size of their remaining German minorities. In the early 1990s the Red Cross estimated that they number roughly 3.2 million, 1.9 million of them in the CIS countries. Statistics show that—partly as a result of legal restrictions—ethnic Germans now almost exclusively immigrate from three CIS countries: Russia, Kazakhstan and Kyrgyzstan (see figure 3.1).

It must be taken into account that, because of more frequent mixed marriages of ethnic Germans living in Russia and Central Asia, future ethnic German immigrants will bring along an unspecified number of non-German spouses and children. It also seems inevitable that as long as political and economic conditions deteriorate in Russia and Central Asia, an increasing number of people will try to declare themselves members of an ethnic German minority in order to have the option of emigrating to Germany in the future.

Migration Between East and West Germany

GDR citizens *(Übersiedler)* were the second major group of German migrants. After the foundation of the GDR in 1949, over 3.8 million East Germans had left their country by the time the Berlin Wall was built in August 1961. During this period, there only was a single year (1959) in which fewer than 200,000 individuals migrated from East to West Germany. The motivation for this stream of migration between the two German states was dissatisfaction with the political system in the GDR, the attractiveness of West Germany during economic booms, and, in many cases, family reunion (Ulrich 1990).

It must be pointed out, however, that from 1949 to August 1961, a total of 393,000 persons also migrated in the opposite direction, from West to East Germany. The annual average was between 25,000 and 40,000 (see figure 3.2). Some of these migrants were members or ideological supporters of West Germany's communist party (KPD), which, as a result of the cold war, was declared illegal in the 1950s.[4] For others, marriage to an East German or family reunion was the main motive.

The yearly loss of inhabitants as a result of emigration caused economic and eventually political destabilization in the GDR. Each bottleneck in supplies and the implementation of socialist redistribution of property (nationalization of even small businesses, collectivization of agriculture) coincided with a higher rate of emigration. After a new rise in east-west migration in 1960–61, the East German government closed the last "hole" in the Iron Curtain by building the Berlin Wall in August 1961. As a consequence, the number of east-west migrants sank to an annual average of 23,000 from 1962 to 1988. The number of

Figure 3.2 Migration Between East and West Germany, 1950–95

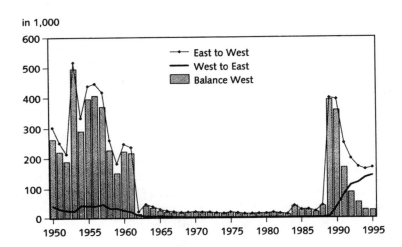

Source: Rudolph 1994 (for 1950–90); data from the Statistisches Bundesamt (for 1991–94).

West Germans moving to East Germany declined on average to 2,600 persons a year (see figure 3.2).

Between August 1961 and late 1988, despite the existence of the Wall and a very restrictive travel regime, almost 600,000 GDR citizens managed to emigrate to the FRG. About half of these were either people who had been freed from prison by the West German government (some 34,000 cases), which paid a certain sum for each of them, or others whose emigration had been individually negotiated (a total of 215,000). The remainder were GDR old-age pensioners, of which most were allowed to travel freely to the West. It was not until 1989, when there were increasingly visible signs of the destabilization of the communist regime, that the number of citizens leaving against the will of the authorities rose once again. Tens of thousands of East German tourists fled to West German embassies in Prague and Budapest and across the Austro-Hungarian border.

After the fall of the Berlin Wall, a mass exodus ensued. In total, about 390,000 people left the GDR in 1989, and another 395,000 departed in 1990. This large number of emigrants was one of the factors precipitating the end of the GDR in 1989–90. After German reunification, the number of German east-west migrants sank noticeably. At the same time, the number of west-east migrants rose: in 1993 only 172,000 people left the former East Germany, but 119,000 moved there from the western parts of the country (net migration balance, –53,000). Between 1989 and 1993 the eastern part of the country (the territory of the former GDR) lost more than 1 million inhabitants to the western parts (east-west migrants: 1.4 million; west-east migrants: 352,000). Another 300,000 East Germans commute daily or weekly to workplaces in West Germany.[5]

Overall, more than a quarter of East Germany's population emigrated between 1949 and 1993. During this period, 5.9 million Germans migrated from east to west, but only 822,000 moved in the opposite direction (see table 3.1).

Special provision was made for East Germans, as well as for ethnic Germans from Central and Eastern Europe and the USSR, in order to facilitate their integration into West German society. This took place in the form of compensation for property left behind, the acknowledgment of pension entitlements, special payments for the establishment of a new household, and other subsidies aimed at integration, as well as education subsidies, language training, professional retraining, and other measures. Public acceptance of these integration programs was promoted in the immediate postwar years. The regulations dating back to this period were mostly maintained until German unification. Even today, special integration measures for ethnic Germans exist. A further peculiarity of ethnic German immigration is the fact that economic cycles and crises in the FRG had almost no influence on these flows. Cold war and détente, the political climate in the countries of origin, and the extent to which the different governments were interested in this group of people or even bought out would-be migrants played a much more important role.

Emigration and Remigration of German Citizens

Since 1945 the focus of public debates has always been on immigration. The considerable numbers of people leaving the country are a less well-known fact. In the nineteenth and early twentieth centuries, Germans emigrated overseas partly for political but mostly for economic reasons. During this period, 7 to 8 million Germans relocated to the United States, Canada, or South America. The wave of emigration only came to an end with the outbreak of World War I and the more restrictive U.S. immigration laws of the 1920s (Bade 1992).

In the 1930s mainly people persecuted by the Nazis for political, racial, or religious reasons emigrated. The destinations of Jews and political emigrants were the European neighbor states, the USA, the Soviet Union, and a number of other overseas countries (Kulischer 1948).

After 1945 economic reasons were again at the forefront of the push and pull factors. Many people attempted to emigrate overseas, wanting to leave destroyed Germany behind. The motivation for some was better career opportunities; for others, it was the desire to escape the atmosphere of political restoration in postwar Germany. Still others married soldiers and staff of the allied forces and later joined them when they returned to their countries of origin, especially the United States.

In the 1960s temporary emigration for the purpose of studying or working abroad became the most important motivation. A growing number of (West) Germans joined multinational companies and international organizations or engaged in development projects or technical and humanitarian aid in third world and former socialist countries. And a continuously growing number of old-age pensioners is moving to Austria, Italy, and Spain.

Between 1954 and 1994 a total of approximately 3.3 million (West) German citizens left the country for a long period of time or even permanently.[6] This amounted to an annual average of 81,000, though in the years prior to 1970 the numbers were slightly higher (103,000 per year), and the same is true for the years since 1989 (98,000 per year). The recent (1988–1994) emigration wave of German citizens is partly a consequence of the large numbers of *Übersiedler* and *Aussiedler* immigrants to West Germany. (West) German citizenship was granted to all of them, but some used Germany only as a transit country on their way to the United States, Canada, Australia, or South Africa, thus appearing in statistics as German emigrants. In addition, the significant reduction of allied forces in Germany (which were never documented in vital and population statistics) led to the emigration of Germans married to foreign soldiers and staff (Schulz 1994).

During the same period (1954–1994) some 2.3 million (West) German citizens immigrated or returned to (West) Germany.[7] Paralleling the emigration of German citizens, this remigration was higher during the fifties and sixties, diminished somewhat during the period 1971–88, and has risen since. As far as its own citizens are concerned, (West) Germany's migration balance with Western Europe and overseas was negative for most years, resulting in a net loss of 1 million people from 1954 to 1994.

Immigration of Foreigners to Germany

Recruitment and the Rotational Model

With the exception of the refugees and expellees of the years 1945–1948, foreigners from Mediterranean countries formed the largest part of West German immigration. From the mid-1950s, the government itself initiated and encouraged this immigration for economic reasons. In its initial phase, it was accounted for in bilateral agreements.

Long before World War II, there were periods in which the immigration of workers from other European countries increased. The census of 1910 indicated 1.3 million foreigners living in Germany, most of them labor migrants. During World War II, Germany's economy and the German military machine could in large part only be kept running with large numbers of foreign workers mostly recruited against their will (Bade 1992; Dohse 1981). By 1944–45, the number of these foreigners working in Germany had risen to almost 8 million (Herbert 1986). In 1945–46 most of them returned or were forced to return to their countries of origin.[8] Others emigrated to Western Europe, Israel, and other countries overseas. Only a few remained in Germany as displaced persons.

In the immediate postwar years, high rates of unemployment impeded the economic and social integration of refugees and expellees. When Germany's export-oriented so-called economic miracle set in during the 1950s, however, demand for labor increased rapidly. Unemployment disappeared, and postwar refugees, expellees, and GDR citizens were integrated into the West German economy (Luettinger 1986).

Despite the large number of expellees and the yearly entry of hundreds of thousands of GDR citizens, workplaces in some West German industries already could not be filled in the mid-1950s. The West German economy thus began to recruit workers in southern Europe. A formal agreement to this end was signed with Italy in 1955. Other recruitment agreements followed: with Spain and Greece in 1960, with Turkey in 1961, with Morocco in 1963, with Portugal in 1964, with Tunisia in 1965, and finally with Yugoslavia in 1968 (Rudolph 1994).

In the beginning, these agreements had little impact. During the 1950s, employment expanded through the reduction of the number of unemployed and the integration of ethnic German immigrants and former GDR citizens. In 1950 there were only about 72,000 foreign workers in the FRG. By 1960, however, this group had increased to 329,000, of which 144,000 were Italians. Employment of foreigners then started to take off seriously in 1960 and accelerated after the construction of the Berlin Wall (see figure 3.3).

Figure 3.3 Migration of Foreigners to and from Germany, 1954–1995 (in millions)

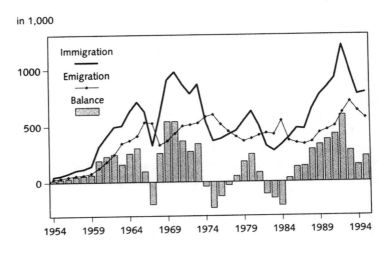

Note: Until 1991, West Germany only.

Source: Data from the Statistisches Bundesamt.

In 1960 for the first time since 1945 the amount of vacancies in West Germany was higher than the number of unemployed. A further decline in the number of German workers was expected, a consequence of demographic development, later entry into the labor market as a result of greater enrollment in higher education, and the declining retirement age. With the export-oriented German economy in full boom, alternatives to the recruitment of foreign labor were hardly discussed: more capital intensity in the coalmining, iron and steel, automobile, and ship building industries would not have brought any immediate relief; increased female participation in the labor force seemed out of the question during this period of restoration of traditional family values (Rudolph 1994); and there was very little reason for West German industry to export work by investing in low-wage countries. Instead, the West German economy stepped up the recruitment of foreign workers. In 1964 the one-millionth foreign worker arrived to a warm welcome.[9] Besides Italy (296,000), Greece (155,000) and Spain (151,000) became the main countries of origin (see figure 3.4). The total number of foreigners in Germany was around 1.2 million in 1964 (2 percent of the total population). By 1970 the number of foreigners had reached 3 million (5 percent of the total population). And in 1973 employment of so-called guest workers reached its peak: 2.6 million, or 12 percent of all gainfully employed people in West Germany. Labor migrants from Turkey (605,000), Yugoslavia (535,000), and Italy (450,000) constituted the largest groups, and a total of almost 4 million foreigners lived in West Germany (7 percent of total population) (see figure 3.5).

The aim of West Germany's recruitment policy was not to foster organized immigration but to counterbalance cyclical and demographic bottlenecks in the West German labor market. Only people who could immediately start to work were welcome and thus recruited. Their work was generally unpleasant and unprestigious and further characterized by lower wages. In contrast to other countries, these wages were fixed after negotiations with German trade unions, which insistent on equal pay for Germans and foreigners. But Germans were no longer interested in such jobs and were hardly willing to fill these vacancies.

As a rule, the work and residence permits issued to recruited foreign laborers were only valid for one year. In the beginning, the temporary character of guest workers' stays and the rota-

Figure 3.4 Foreigners and Foreign Labor in Germany, 1960–1994 (in millions)

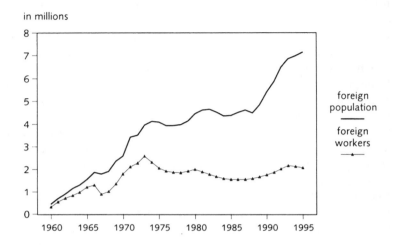

Note: Until 1990, West Germany only.

Source: Amtliche Nachrichten der Bundesanstalt für Arbeit; data from Statistisches Bundesamt

tion of the foreign workforce were questioned neither by the German public and business circles nor by the guest workers and their home countries. This setup not only explains the high level of immigration and remigration in the 1960s and early 1970s (see figure 3.3) but also the low degree of opposition in the receiving society to this mass migration of foreign labor.

In the GDR a not-too-different model was introduced later. In order to meet its chronic labor shortage in the 1970s, East Germany recruited workers from other socialist countries in Central and Eastern Europe and later also from Cuba, Mozambique, and Vietnam. But in contrast to their West German counterparts, the GDR authorities strictly insisted on compulsory rotation (Dorbritz and Speigner 1990). Almost all labor immigrants were forced to return to their countries of origin when the contracted period was over. From the quantitative point of view, however, employment of foreigners in the GDR never played the role it did in the FRG. Even in the late 1980s the number of foreigners did not exceed 200,000 (1.2 percent of the population).

Figure 3.5 Foreign Labor in Germany by Selected nationalities, 1954–1994 (in thousands)

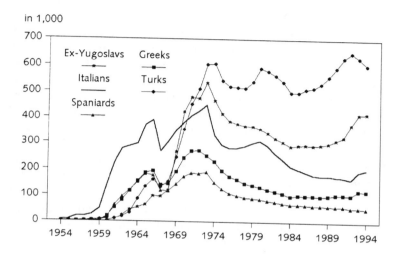

Note: Until 1990, West Germany only.

Source: Rudolph 1994; Bericht 1995; Arbeitsmarkt 1994.

From 1954 to 1965 the average number of foreigners immigrating to the FRG annually surpassed that of foreigners leaving the country by 136,000. As a consequence of the recession of 1966–67, however, the number of foreigners immigrating to Germany declined noticeably, while the number of those remigrating to their home countries increased. West Germany's migration balance, positive (97,000) in 1966, became negative (–198,000) in 1967.

During this period, the heavy influence of business cycles on the immigration and remigration of foreign labor was apparent. When the next boom period started in 1968, the migration balance again became positive as a result of further labor recruitment. From 1968 to 1973, more foreigners than ever came to West Germany. Every day some five hundred to a thousand new guest workers were recruited, bringing the surplus of foreign immigrants to 387,000 a year. Sometimes trains and planes had to be chartered in order to bring enough additional workers into the country. The foreign population grew from 1.9 to 4.0 million, and the number of foreign workers and employees increased from 1.1 million to its historical peak of 2.6 million (1973) (see figure 3.5).

Starting in the late 1960s, the rotational model, well accepted at first, began to lose ground. Many labor migrants were not able to save as much money within one or two years as they had hoped. West German employers, forced constantly to revolve their foreign staff, no longer wanted to keep recruiting and training new workers just because the work and residence permits of those recruited earlier had expired. The governments of some countries of origin began to voice criticisms, as did German trade unions, employers, and other groups. The West German government reacted by easing restrictions on the renewal of residence permits. Beginning in 1971 labor migrants who had worked in Germany for at least five years could claim special work permits valid for another five years. For many foreigners, this change improved their legal status. One consequence was increased family reunification. A growing number of spouses and children of foreign labor migrants moved to Germany. The ability of the German authorities to regulate immigration according to the demands of the labor market was thus strongly reduced.

The Recruitment Stop, Attempted Consolidation, New Waves of Immigration

The year 1973 brought a dramatic turn in Germany's migration history. First, even before the first oil price shock and the ensuing recession, the government tripled the fees that employers had to pay for the recruitment of foreign labor. (Other European countries also stopped or limited foreign recruitment during this period: Switzerland, under pressure from xenophobic right-wing movements, in 1970; Sweden in 1972; and France in 1974.) Then, in October 1973, just after the OPEC oil embargo, the West German government announced the end of foreign recruitment altogether. Some channels of legal immigration to Germany remained, notably family reunion (with children less than sixteen years old and spouses) and asylum. New channels have also emerged, provided for in regulations governing the admission of quota refugees; seasonal and contract workers; and managers and specialists working for multinational and foreign companies doing business in Germany, correspondents of foreign media, artists, and foreign students. In addition, citizens of EU countries and, since 1 January 1994, citizens of countries belonging to the European Economic Area (EEA)[10] may work and live anywhere they choose within the EU and EEA.

The recruitment stop was part of a package aimed at consolidating and decreasing foreign employment in Germany. Other measures were meant to promote either remigration to the country of origin or social integration in Germany. But although the package eventually limited the number of new immigrants, in the medium term it did not have the desired results. In fact, the measures had some unexpected side effects (see Bade 1994a; Höhn and Rein 1990).

During the recession of 1974–75 immigration decreased and remigration increased slightly. The balance of migration remained negative from 1974 to 1977. The total number of foreigners decreased by a mere 200,000, but the number of foreign laborers by 706,000, dropping to 1.9 million in 1977. This development did not continue, however. As early as 1976 the annual number of newly arriving foreign immigrants started to increase again, while fewer foreigners left the country. In 1978 the balance was positive by 50,000, in 1979 by 180,000, and in 1980 by 246,000 (see figure 3.3). In 1980 4.5 million foreigners lived in the FRG (7 percent of the total population). Foreigners in the workforce numbered 2.1 million, particularly laborers from Turkey (592,000), Yugoslavia (357,000), and Italy (309,000; see figure 3.4). In the following years, the number of foreigners hardly declined (4.4 million in 1985) despite the recession of the early 1980s, even though the number of foreign workers sank noticeably (to 1.6 million in 1985). In 1983–84 the German government tried to promote remigration of labor migrants by offering financial incentives, and from 1982 to 1984 West Germany's net migration balance for foreigners was indeed negative (–470,000). But from 1985 to 1987, the balance once again became positive (see figure 3.3).

The declining employment of foreigners during this period had several causes, among them a slower rate of economic growth and the entry of West Germany's baby boomers into the labor market. There was also a massive reduction of jobs in those economic sectors and branches where most foreigners were employed (Münz and Ulrich 1993).

A new wave of immigration set in after 1987, spurred by a rise in the number of applicants for asylum (see figure 3.6), the fall of the Iron Curtain, war and ethnic cleansing in former Yugoslavia, and the mounting pressure on the Kurds in south-eastern Turkey. Ethnic conflicts and bloodshed in former Yugoslavia and southeastern Turkey increased not only the number of asylum seekers but regular migration as well. Many foreign workers originating from these regions chose to bring remaining family members to Germany.

Apart from a variety of push factors there was a distinct pull factor: the short economic boom in 1990–91, sparked by debt-financed German unification, also led to a new wave of immigration of foreign labor. This involved not only foreign labor from Turkey and former Yugoslavia but also, for the first time since 1945, labor migrants from Poland, the Czech Republic, Hungary, and the like who came to Germany as seasonal workers on a contract basis—employed, for example, as harvesters—or in order to receive professional training (Rudolph 1994; Velling 1994).

In 1988 4.5 million foreigners were living in West Germany. By 1994 their number had increased to 7 million. Foreigners employed in Germany, however, only increased from 1.6 to 2.2 million during the same time (see figure 3.5). A breakdown by nationality shows that the largest groups of foreign workers and employees are still those from Turkey (605,000 in 1994) and from former Yugoslavia (420,900), both matching their 1973/74 highs in 1992–94. In contrast, the number of workers from Italy (202,500), Greece (118,600), and Spain (52,600) is markedly lower than it was twenty years ago (see figure 3.5).

Asylum Seekers and Refugees

Article 16 of the German Constitution *(Grundgesetz)* states: "Persons persecuted for political reasons have the right to asylum." Until 1993, this meant applicants possessed an individual and personal right to be granted asylum if they were able to prove persecution, a fairly generous condition compared to that in other countries. This stipulation had been included in light of

Germany's Nazi past and the fact that some politicians of the postwar era had survived the period from 1933 to 1945 in exile.

Between 1953 and 1978 a total of 178,000 asylum seekers arrived in the FRG (an average of 7,100 per annum). The numbers increased in the short term in 1956, after the suppression of the Hungarian uprising, and in 1968/69, after the Soviet invasion of Czechoslovakia. As a result of the last military coup in Turkey (1980) and the introduction of martial law in Poland (1980/81), a further 200,000 applications for asylum were filed between 1979 and 1981. The federal government reacted by implementing administrative restrictions. After more than ten years of visa-free travel to Germany, Turkish citizens again had to apply for visas. This measure was maintained for Poles and many fewer visas were issued, despite the imposition of martial law. The number of asylum seekers from the two countries immediately decreased by almost 90 percent (see figure 3.6).

Figure 3.6 Asylum Seekers in Germany, 1970–1995

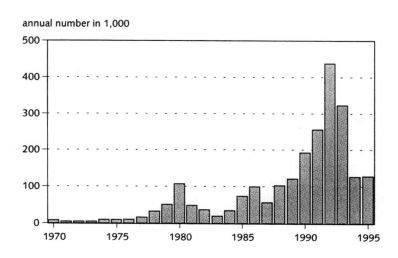

Source: Data from the Statistisches Bundesamt.

The number of applications for asylum did not again rise above 40,000 a year until the mid-1980s, with the exception of the years 1979 through 1981. Then, beginning in 1985, conflicts and crises such as the outbreak of civil war in Sri Lanka and the persecution of the Tamil minority (in 1985) and, later on (from 1991/92 to 1995), war and ethnic cleansing in former Yugoslavia (mainly in Croatia and Bosnia but also in Serbian Voyvodina and Kosovo) led to an increased influx of refugees into Germany. Some analysts regard this as further evidence that push factors take precedence over pull factors (Bade 1994a). Statistics show that, whatever the motivations behind immigration were and are, the main gates of entry shifted from labor migration to family unification and asylum: in the early 1970s the share of asylum seekers was below 1 percent of total foreign immigration to Germany; in the early 1990s it reached levels above 30 percent (see table 3.3).

After the annual number of asylum seekers had surpassed 100,000 in the late 1980s, the inflow of immigrants and the possibilities to reduce it became a central issue for German domestic policy. It was stressed that a large portion of asylum seekers did not suffer from political persecution but instead came for economic reasons. There is hardly any doubt that economic interests formed part of the motivation of some of these would-be immigrants. Discussions about the size of this group in Germany have been influenced by the low rate of recognition of applications. Until 1980 the rate of recognition was over 80 percent, to a large extent because of the cold war. In 1985 the rate was still 29 percent. In the early 1990s, however, only 3 to 7 percent of applicants were granted asylum, in most cases after an administrative procedure lasting several months and sometimes even years. With the asylum regulations in force since mid-1993 the legal procedure for decision making was speeded up, while at the same time the numbers of applicants were reduced. In 1992 the number of new applicants was twice as high as the number of decisions made. In 1994 the stock of undecided cases was reduced substantially. For every new applicant in 1994 almost three decisions were made, and that share increased again: in 1994 some 20 percent and in 1995 14 percent of all applicants were given the desired refugee status. This does not mean, however, that the rejected applicants must all be classified as spurious refugees or economic migrants.

Table 3.3 Asylum Seekers and Regular Foreign Migrants,
1970–94

Year[1]	Immigration of Foreigners Number in thousands (1)	Migration balance of foreigners Number in thousands (2)	Asylum seekers Number in thousands (3)	As a percentage of all foreign immigrants[2] (4)
1970	976.2	541.6	8.6	0.9
1971	870.7	370.5	5.4	0.6
1972	787.2	272.7	5.3	0.7
1973	869.1	342.3	5.6	0.6
1974	542.4	−39.5	9.4	1.7
1975	367.3	−233.1	9.6	2.6
1976	388.2	−127.4	11.1	2.9
1977	423.5	−28.7	16.4	3.9
1978	456.7	50.7	33.1	7.3
1979	545.9	179.8	51.5	9.4
1980	632.3	246.3	107.8	17.1
1981	502.0	86.2	49.4	9.8
1982	322.4	−111.4	37.4	11.6
1983	276.4	−148.7	19.7	7.1
1984	333.3	−213.2	35.3	10.6
1985	400.0	32.2	73.8	18.5
1986	479.5	131.5	99.7	20.8
1987	473.3	139.1	57.4	12.1
1988	648.6	289.5	103.1	15.9
1989	770.8	332.5	121.3	15.7
1990	842.4	376.3	193.1	22.9
1991	920.5	423.0	256.1	27.8
1992	1,207.6	592.9	438.2	36.3
1993	986.9	276.6	322.6	32.7
1994	773.9	252.5	127.2	16.4

1. Until 1988, West Germany only; in 1989–90, East and West Germany; since 1991: unified Germany.
2. Asylum seekers are immediately registered for the statistics in col. 3) but enter immigration statistics (col. 1) only with a time lag, therefore col. 4 is only a rough estimate for individual years.

The data include regular foreign immigrants and asylum seekers but not GDR citizens and other ethnic Germans.

Source: Data from the Statistisches Bundesamt.

The German procedure for granting or denying asylum only recognizes cases of individual persecution and human rights abuses if they were of a clearly political nature and carried out by representatives of the state of origin. This means that, today, a simple threat to life and freedom caused by civil war, terror, or torture practices accepted within the country of origin no longer confers a right to political asylum. But many applicants who have not been granted status as political refugees are tolerated in Germany or at least not sent back to their countries of origin, in consideration of the current circumstances there. This practice of nonrefoulement is codified in the Geneva Convention on Refugees in the ban on the expulsion of such individuals.

Others have engaged in litigation against the denial of their refugee status and had their negative decisions overturned. Estimates indicate that until 1993 about one-fifth to one-third of all applicants belonged to this category (Bade 1994a). In the last years some 15 to 20 percent of all unsuccessful applicants have been forced to leave Germany. Larger numbers have returned more or less voluntarily to their home countries. Others left Germany for a third country. But more than two out of three asylum seekers in the years 1985 through 1993 stayed in Germany (Schulz 1994).

According to estimates by the German Ministry of the Interior, in 1994 more than 1.7 million refugees and asylum seekers were living in Germany (*Bericht* 1995). The largest group (650,000) were de facto refugees who had not been granted political asylum but were tolerated for humanitarian and political reasons. The second-largest group (415,000 in 1994) consisted of asylum seekers whose applications were still under consideration. Another group comprises victims of (civil) war and ethnic cleansing, for which since 1 July 1993 an amendment to the law on foreigners has created the possibility of temporary protection without examination of the individual case. Between 1993 and 1995 this status was granted to some 350,000 persons, mainly Muslims from Bosnia. Since 1996 Germany and Bosnia have tried to repatriate these Muslim refugees. Only 267,000 recognized political refugees and their families were entitled to permanent residence in Germany in 1994.[11] Quota refugees, individuals who have been granted political asylum elsewhere and were accepted into Germany within the framework of international burden sharing or for particular humanitarian reasons, are entitled to permanent residence permits; they account for a small share of all recognized refugees (67,200). Jews from the former Soviet Union are also accepted as quota refugees in Germany without having to prove any individual persecution. Between 1990 and 1995 some 48,000 (ex-) Soviet Jews were allowed to immigrate. Another 110,000 have applied at German embassies in the successor states to the Soviet Union.[12] The statistics on asylum seekers and refugees also include a group of 20,600 persons who have been denied status as political refugees but cannot be repatriated because they are stateless.

The sharp increase in the number of asylum seekers between 1988 and 1992 and the large amount of total immigration during that same period led to fierce political debate over an amendment to German asylum law and the German Constitution that would restrict access to political asylum. The ruling conservative parties (CDU/CSU) and other conservative groups were mainly interested in limiting the further immigration of asylum seekers (and other foreigners). The oppositional Social Democrats (SPD) and some of the Liberal Democrats (FDP, a coalition party of the CDU) sought a package of regulations combining measures on legal immigration, social integration, and naturalization. In 1993 these debates resulted in a change in the asylum law (Blahusch 1994; Bade 1994b). The possibility of applying for asylum was limited in two ways. First, applicants who have entered Germany via other states belonging to the EU or any other so-called safe country (the Czech Republic, Poland, Switzerland) can be forced to return to that country. Second, a simplified recognition procedure was introduced for asylum seekers from so-called states with no persecution; in most cases this leads to immediate rejection of the application and possible expulsion (on the recent changes to asylum law, see Kay Hailbronner, "New Techniques for Rendering Asylum Manageable," ch. 4 in vol. 4 of this series).

Because Germany is surrounded by safe countries, all of them signatories to the Geneva Convention, asylum seekers can only apply when arriving by air, by sea, or through another entry not related to one of the surrounding safe countries or if the transit country from which they entered Germany cannot be identified. In addition to the revision of the asylum law, bilateral readmission agreements were signed with Romania (1992), Poland (1993), Switzerland (1993), Bulgaria (1994), the Czech Republic (1994), and Vietnam (1995). Some of these agreements only regulate the readmission of nationals from these countries. Other countries, such as Poland, have also agreed to take back citizens of third countries who entered Germany illegally via their border with Germany or who have been denied asylum in Germany after having crossed this border. From 1993 to 1995 Germany paid DM 120 million to cover parts of Poland's additional expenditures for tighter border control and the subsidizing of rejected immigrants. Similar payments were made to the Czech Republic (DM 60 million). Romania has received financial compensation for taking back Romanian asylum seekers, most of them of Gypsy origin.[13]

Modification of the German Constitution and the more restrictive procedures obviously had the intended effect: In the second half of 1993, the number of applications was already lower than before. Between January and June 1993, 224,000 applications were filed; between July and December 1993, the number decreased to 98,000. And in the entire year of 1994, only 127,200 individuals were able to apply for asylum in Germany. Almost exactly the same number (127,900) applied for asylum in 1995. In addition to this decrease, some side effects of the new regulation are already visible. For one thing, it seems that a diversion of asylum seekers to neighboring European countries has taken place; the Netherlands and the countries of East Central Europe have registered a significant increase in applications for asylum since the new German regulations came into effect (Bade 1994a). Some observers have also diagnosed a shift from (statistically visible) legal asylum seekers to illegal immigration to Germany (Blahusch 1994; Winkler 1994).

Structure and Situation of Foreigners in Germany

From Guest Workers to Immigrants

Postwar refugees, GDR citizens, and other ethnic Germans came to West Germany with a clear perspective: to settle here and to stay for good. In contrast, the first generation of foreign labor migrants planned to earn money and then return home. Calling them "guest workers" made sense. This could be the main reason that Germans at the time did not challenge the recruitment of several million foreigners. The so-called guest workers not only filled gaps in the labor market and jobs Germans didn't want but also served to buffer against fluctuations in the business cycle without having to be integrated.

During the economic recession of 1966–67, many unemployed guest workers moved back to their home countries only to return to Germany when the economy recovered. After the recruitment stop, however, foreigners from non-EC/EU countries, hence particularly Turkish and Yugoslav nationals,[14] could not count on being able to reenter the country after returning home. For this reason, many of them stayed in the Germany in spite of being unemployed during the recession phases of 1974–75 and 1981–84 (see figures 3.3 and 3.5).

The intention of the recruitment stop was to reduce the number of foreigners in Germany, but unintended side effects led to the opposite. Until the mid-1970s, the foreigners themselves had adhered to the concept of staying temporarily in Germany. Now they knew that they either had to stay in Germany or to leave the country with no chance of returning during the next economic boom. This inevitably changed the structure of migration (Seifert 1995).

Until 1973–74 mainly younger men between twenty and forty years of age had come to West Germany. From the mid-1970s on, more and more of them brought their families (spouses and children) to Germany or established new families here. There is no precise information on the number of foreign immigrants who came to Germany by way of family reunion. Some authors (Velling 1993a; Franz 1991; Schmidt and Zimmermann 1992) estimate that family reunion accounted for more than half of the immigration in the 1970s and 1980s. Using the German Socioeconomic Panel (GSOEP), Velling analyzed the determinants influencing foreigners to bring their families to Germany. The probability of family reunion was highest among the Spanish population in Germany. It increased with higher age and longer residence. Family reunion was often postponed during phases of general unemployment in Germany. The percentage of married foreigners living in Germany without their spouses declined from over 80 percent in the early 1960s to below 20 percent in the early 1980s.

With increased family reunion and the formation of new families in Germany, the rotational model became obsolete. This is also reflected in the increasing duration of foreigners' stays in Germany (see figure 3.7). By the end of 1994 half of all foreigners had been in Germany for over ten years, and one in four had been here for more than twenty. Only about 30 percent of all foreigners had entered the country less than 4 years before. Of the 7 million foreign nationals living in Germany, 1.2 million were born in this country. There are varying patterns for different nationalities, however. The Portuguese were among the first guest-worker nationalities. The majority of those living today in Germany has been in the country for more then ten years. However, the share of Portuguese with shorter stays in Germany has increased. Turks, too, belong to one of the nationalities that have long been settled in Germany. More than two out of three have already spent more then ten years in the country. For the Poles, the corresponding share is only 21 percent; instead, the majority of them arrived in Germany at the end of the 1980s or later. And in case of Bosnia, the impact of the wave of immigration during the civil war (1992–95) is apparent, although the share of Bosnians who are long-term residents of Germany might be understated because some of them are still counted as Yugoslav nationals in the German Foreigners Register.

Today there can be no doubt: what started as temporary labor migration in the 1950s and 1960s has turned into regular immigration to Germany, not intended but made possible by the existing legal regulations. Most foreign labor migrants now live here with their families. They will stay in Germany until they retire, if not for the rest of their lives, and many of them will be buried here some day.

Origins of Foreigners

Between 1954 and 1994 21.9 million foreigners arrived in Germany, but 15.6 million left the country during the same period. The range of countries of origin has become more diversified since the early 1970s. Until then, more than 50 percent of the foreigners came from countries belonging (then or now) to the

Figure 3.7 Foreign Nationals in Germany by Duration of Stay, 1994 (percentages by duration of stay)

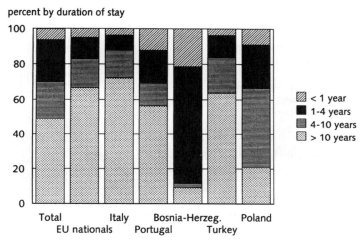

Source: Data from the Statistisches Bundesamt.

EC/EU, most of them from Italy, Greece, Spain, or Austria. In the 1970s other nations made up a higher share of annual immigration (see figure 3.8). In 1970 Turkish and Yugoslav nationals became the two largest groups, outnumbering the Italians (see figure 3.9). In 1994, EU nationals accounted for a quarter of foreigners living in Germany. Turkish nationals (2 million) now are by far the largest group. They represent 28 percent of the foreign population living in Germany. Second are the citizens of former Yugoslavia (18 percent, of which many are victims of war under temporary protection), followed by Italians (8 percent) and Greeks (5 percent). The percentage of Poles has recently grown to 4 percent (see figure 3.9).

In the 1960s and early 1970s most foreigners had only been living in Germany for a short time or were planning only temporary stays. The recruitment agreement with Turkey mentioned a maximum residence of two years, with subsequent rotation. As early as the second half of the 1960s, however, this principle was no longer enforced very strictly. After 1971 non-EU nationals who had worked in Germany for more than five years became entitled to apply for a work permit for another five years.

Figure 3.8 Structure of Gross Immigration of Foreigners to Germany, 1960–95 (in thousands)

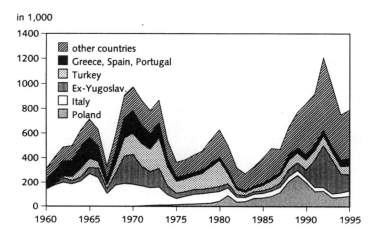

Source: Data from the Statistisches Bundesamt.

Today nationals of other EU and EEA countries (25 percent of all foreigners) have the best legal status. They may enter Germany freely, establish legal residence, and work here without special permission.[15] Other foreigners have a more or less secure status. They may be only tolerated[16] or have temporary residence permits, or they may possess a permanent right of residence.

Regional Distribution of Foreigners in Germany

Some 75 percent of all foreigners live in only four of the sixteen federal provinces *(Länder):* Baden-Württemberg, Bavaria, Hesse, and North Rhine–Westphalia (see table 3.4). This regional concentration is mostly the result of economic structures and the subsequent job opportunities for foreigners. In certain areas, the housing market and the ethnic communities or networks that have established themselves in many cities also play a role as additional pull factors. Only asylum seekers are distributed among the *Länder* according to a system in order to foster regional burden sharing (Bucher, Kocks, and Siedhoff 1992; Schulz 1994).

Figure 3.9 Foreign Nationals in Germany by Citizenship, 1971 and 1994

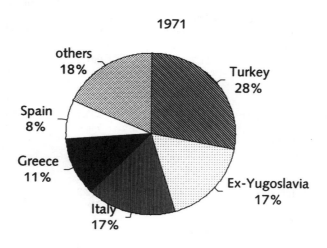

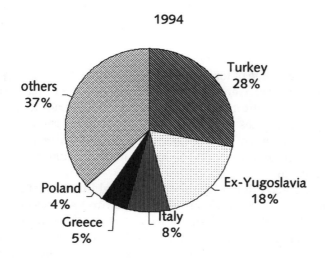

Note: For 1994, "Ex-Yugoslavia" includes Bosnia-Herzegovina, Croatia, Macedonia, Montenegro, Serbia, and Slovenia.

Source: Data from the Statistisches Bundesamt.

Table 3.4 Share of Foreign Population by *Länder,* 1993

Federal Provinces	Total Population Number in thousands	Foreigners Number in thousands	As a percentage of total population
Baden-Württemberg	10,148.7	1,190.8	11.7
Bavaria	11,770.3	991.9	8.4
Berlin	3,465.7	385.9	11.0
Brandenburg	2,542.7	55.0	2.2
Bremen	685.8	75.7	11.0
Hamburg	1,688.8	235.5	13.9
Hesse	5,922.6	745.6	12.6
Mecklenburg–Lower Pomerania	1,865.0	22.5	1.2
Lower Saxony	7,577.5	425.8	5.6
North Rhine–Westphalia	17,679.2	1,812.3	10.3
Rhineland-Palatinate	3,881.0	258.9	6.7
Saarland	1,084.0	68.2	6.3
Saxony	4,641.0	50.8	1.1
Saxony-Anhalt	2,797.0	33.9	1.2
Schleswig-Holstein	2,679.6	125.9	4.7
Thuringia	2,545.8	20.3	0.8

Source: *Bericht* 1995.

The percentage of foreigners is highest in large urban agglomerations in West Germany with a large share of coal-mining, iron and steel, automobile, and chemical industries and highly specialized services. This is particularly true for the industrialized parts of Baden-Württemberg, the greater Munich area, the Rhine-Main area, the Cologne area, the Ruhr, and West Berlin (see table 3.5).

In 1992, according to data of the Federal Institute of Regional Studies and Planning (Bundesanstalt für Landeskunde und Raumordnung), more than 60 percent of the foreigners in Germany lived in big cities or other densely populated regions (Göddecke-Stellmann 1994). In contrast, only 41 percent of German nationals lived in such areas. While the share of foreigners among the rural population is less than 5 percent, it is 10 to 30 percent in the larger cities, for example, it is over 20 percent in Frankfurt-am-Main, Stuttgart, and Munich, about three times the national average (see table 3.5).

Table 3.5 German Cities with the Highest Share of Foreign
Population, 1993

Cities	Foreign Population in thousands	as a percentage of total population
Frankfurt-am-Main	184.4	27.9
Stuttgart	139.5	23.3
Munich	279.7	22.3
Cologne	174.3	18.1
Ludwigshafen	30.0	17.9
Düsseldorf	99.7	17.2
Duisburg	88.1	16.3
Augsburg	42.6	16.1
Wiesbaden	42.3	15.8
Hamburg	235.5	13.9
Berlin	385.9	11.1
Germany	6878.1	8.6

Source: *Bericht* 1995.

The percentage of foreign nationals in East Germany (1.5
percent in 1989) declined immediately after the collapse of the
GDR but soon increased again to its former level (to 1.5 percent
in 1993, excluding East Berlin). Most of the contract workers
recruited by the GDR have returned to their countries of origin
or moved to West Germany. The only remaining group comprises Vietnamese nationals not readmitted by their government. As a rule, immigration to East Germany today is not a
result of favorable economic conditions but a function of the federal distribution of asylum seekers and victims of war (mainly
Bosnians) under temporary protection (until 1996/97). East
Berlin has also experienced a considerable inflow of Jews from
the former Soviet Union who have been admitted into Germany
as quota refugees. Some foreigners already established in the
western part of the city have also moved to East Berlin and its
suburbs. The only percentages of foreign population worth men-
tioning are those of East Berlin (4 percent in 1993) and Brandenburg (2 percent). The share of foreigners in the urban
agglomerations of Halle-Leipzig, Dresden, and Rostock (1.6 to
1.9 percent) is also higher than the East German average.

Employment of Foreigners by Economic Sectors and Branches

Today, the most significant differences between Germans and foreigners exist on the labor market. In 1992 56 percent of foreign workers but only 16 percent of their German counterparts were in unskilled or semiskilled positions. A far lower proportion of foreigners as compared to Germans have moved into white-collar jobs. This shows that in spite of nominal equality, most foreign immigrants, even after having worked in Germany for extended periods of time, are not able to improve their positions, whether by changing employers and jobs or by climbing the career ladder within the same company. Many of them are or were only able to work in Germany if they were willing to accept unattractive and poorly paid blue-collar jobs demanding few qualifications. This is why many were and still are employed by German industry and in the service sector (Meis 1993; Seifert 1995).

In the early 1970s two-thirds of all foreigners worked in manufacturing and construction. Because employing them was relatively cheap, companies were able to postpone rationalization; even marginal producers and less productive sectors were able to survive, at least for a certain time, thanks to cheap foreign labor. But over the period 1974–94, workplaces filled by foreigners have disproportionately disappeared or moved to low-wage countries in Southeast Asia and Central Europe (Czech Republic, Hungary, Poland). By the early 1990s no more than half the foreigners working in Germany were employed in manufacturing and construction. Instead, many of them had switched to services (e.g., health and care, cleaning, catering, tourism; see Rudolph 1994; Seifert 1995).

In 1994 only 9.4 percent of all people gainfully employed in Germany were foreign nationals (compared to 12 percent in 1973). They continue to be concentrated in certain sectors of the economy (see figure 3.10). Their representation is above average in the restaurant and hotel industries and in tourism in general (29.6 percent in 1993) as well as in the iron and steel industry, especially in casting (23.4 percent in 1994) and automobile production (13.2 percent in 1994). Other sectors in which the percentage of foreigners is above average are forestry and agriculture (12.8 percent in 1994), because of a large share of foreign seasonal workers, and construction (13.7 percent in 1994), as a result of the growing number of foreign contract workers.[17] In these two sectors, it is likely that much more foreign labor is involved than official statistics show. The same goes for personal services in households (Münz and Ulrich 1993; Seifert 1995).

Figure 3.10 Absolute Size and Share of Foreign Labor by Branches, 1994

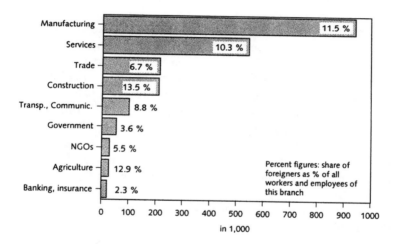

Note: The percentages show the share of foreigners as a percentage of all workers and employees in the given sector.

Source: *Bericht* 1995

But not only the number of foreign cleaners, nannies, cooks, and florists has risen in the last few years. There are also more foreign employers and self-employed persons in trade, business, and industry: approximately 239,000 at present. Some foreign entrepreneurs have specialized in products or services unique to their ethnic communities; others trade in products from their native countries or make use of business links back home. However, for far more than half of them, ethnic background has no bearing on their business endeavors, and thus they perform on an equal footing with their German counterparts.

Rainer Münz and *Ralf Ulrich*

Naturalization of Foreigners

It is a characteristic of Germany as a self-declared nonimmigration country that the naturalization of foreign immigrants and their children is still the exception, not the rule. Foreign nationals are entitled to discretionary naturalization after more than ten years of residence. For children who have grown up in Germany, a minimum of eight years of residence (and attendance of German schools) is required. In contrast, ethnic German immigrants have immediate access to German citizenship on entering the country.

Between 1974 and 1992 only 311,000 discretionary naturalizations took place (see table 3.6). A mere 0.3 to 0.6 percent of foreigners living in Germany were naturalized annually. By international standards, this rate was very low. This is mainly due to the fact that German citizenship is closely linked to descent and ethnic origin (jus sanguinis), which hinders the automatic or simplified naturalization of children born in Germany to foreigners. Significant changes were made in 1993, however, and the number of naturalizations increased to 74,000 that same year (1 percent of foreigners living in Germany; see table 3.6).

The naturalization rate is still low, however, given that more than half the foreigners living in Germany fulfill the criterion of a minimum residence of at least ten years (or eight years, for children). The other criteria foreigners are required to meet are proof of good conduct, permanent domicile, and guaranteed income in Germany. The last excludes foreigners living on welfare benefits or receiving unemployment benefits. The large majority of foreigners also fulfill these conditions. Still, most of them neither applied for citizenship nor, until very recently, were actively encouraged to do so by the German authorities. Until the mid-1980s, high administrative fees of (DM 5,000, approx. US $3,500) were an obstacle.

One step toward easier access to naturalization was made with changes in the foreigners law (Ausländergesetz) in 1993. Foreigners between sixteen and twenty-three years of age with eight or more years of residency in Germany and foreigners above the age of twenty-three with a minimum of fifteen years of residency (about 40 percent of foreigners) now have a legal claim

to naturalization comparable to that of ethnic German immigrants *(Anspruchseinbürgerung)*. The fees for this procedure are
now small (DM 100, approximately US $65). This new legal
channel has been used especially by older foreigners. In 1993
more than 29,000 foreigners were naturalized on the basis of the
new regulations, in addition to 44,900 naturalizations of foreigners based on discretionary decision of German authorities
(Ermessenseinbürgerungen).

Table 3.6 Naturalization of Ethnic German Immigrants
(Aussiedler) and Foreigners, 1974–1993

	Ethnic Germans *(Aussiedler)*	Foreigners	
	absolute numbers	absolute numbers	As a percentage of foreign population
1974	12,256	12,488	0.3
1975	14,198	10,727	0.3
1976	16,347	13,134	0.3
1977	18,097	13,535	0.3
1978	18,635	14,075	0.4
1979	19,780	15,172	0.4
1980	22,034	14,969	0.3
1981	22,235	13,643	0.3
1982	26,014	13,266	0.3
1983	25,151	14,334	0.3
1984	23,351	14,695	0.3
1985	21,019	13,894	0.3
1986	22,616	14,030	0.3
1987	23,781	14,029	0.3
1988	30,123	16,660	0.4
1989	50,794	17,742	0.4
1990	81,140	20,237	0.4
1991	114,335	27,295	0.5
1992	142,862	37,042	0.6
1993	154,493	74,058 [1]	1.0

1. This includes naturalization by discretionary decision of German
   authorities *(Ermessenseinbürgerungen)* and naturalization based on a
   legal claim *(Anspruchseinbürgerungen)*, according to sections 85 and 86
   of the foreigners' law (Ausländergesetz).

Source: *Bericht* 1995; data from the Statistisches Bundesamt.

In the 1990s integrating elements of jus soli and allowing multiple citizenship are key topics in the policy discussion on naturalization. For many foreigners, especially for the second generation, born in Germany, the legal framework of foreigners law *(Ausländerrecht)* does not really apply to their actual situations. Moreover, their legal status, especially the perceived possibility of deportation, is an obstacle to their full integration into German society.

Focusing on legal regulations, however, it should not be ignored that naturalization is also a result of perceived advantages and disadvantages for eligible foreigners and therefore depends on reliable information and communication among local authorities, immigrant communities, and the immigrants themselves. According to a MARPLAN survey (see *Bericht* 1995), among Spaniards, Italians, (ex-)Yugoslavs, Greeks, and Turks living in Germany in 1994, only one in two was interested in acquiring German citizenship. About 20 percent were very interested in naturalization. Younger foreigners expressed more interest than did older foreigners. In part, this reflects discouragement stemming from the more difficult and expensive access to German citizenship in the past. In addition, some foreigners with permanent residence status feel they would gain little by becoming German citizens. Often foreigners are simply not informed about their legal rights regarding naturalization and permanent residency status.

This sometimes leads to unacceptable individual hardships, for example, when foreigners neglect to apply for permanent residency status even though they have a legal claim after decades of living and working in Germany. When such individuals reach pensionable age, if they apply for public benefits (to supplement pensions below the subsistence level), they risk expulsion. In the current policy discussion, some demand that the relevant German government agencies be obliged to inform foreigners about their rights and legal claims and to encourage naturalization actively through nationwide campaigns.

Although perceived as an exception, multiple citizenship has become more common in Germany in recent years. In 1993 almost 30,000 naturalizations of foreigners (40 percent of the total) involved the acceptance of multiple citizenship. For applicants of some nationalities, whose countries of origin arbitrarily complicate or even deny release from previous citizenship, the percentage of naturalizations with acceptance of multiple citizenship was even higher (in 1993, 89 percent of naturalizations from Afghanistan, 87 percent of those from Morocco, and 68 percent of those from Turkey).

Naturalization does not necessarily guarantee or even facilitate social integration. This is a bitter experience that naturalized immigrants and their children, as well as many ethnic Germans from Eastern Europe and Central Asia, have faced. Nevertheless, in view of the size of the foreign population and its share of the total population, it is vital that policy address the question of citizenship. If government, institutions, and political parties cater mainly to the interests of their constituencies, then 7 million foreigners are not only excluded from most forms of political representation but also have much smaller opportunities to fight for resources and defend their special interests. This is particularly obvious at the municipal level, especially in those large West German cities in which one in five or even one in four inhabitants has no German passport. As the foreign population is likely to increase in the coming decades—not just through immigration but as a result of children born as foreigners in Germany—the question of naturalization or the introduction of elements of jus soli will become even more acute.

Demography and Politics

A New Phase of Immigration to Germany?

In the late 1980s and early 1990s the total number of immigrants exceeded those of previous peak periods (e.g., 1969–70). Between 1988 and 1994 a total of 8.3 million ethnic Germans, asylum seekers, and regular foreign immigrants came to Germany, an annual average of 1.2 million. At the same time, 4.3 million people left the country (an annual average of 623,000). This led to a positive migration balance of 4 million for the period from 1988 to 1994. This positive balance was largely due to the influx of *Aussiedler*, asylum seekers, new labor migrants, and family members of already established labor migrants, which accounted for a net migration balance of 2.4 million for foreigners (averaging more than 349,000 annually from 1988 through 1994) and of 1.5 million for ethnic Germans and German citizens (averaging more than 221,000 annually over the same period; see table 3.7). During this period, the USA, the classic immigrant society, was the only other country in the world with a similar amount of immigration. One major difference remains: the United States has more than three times the population and more than twenty-five times the territory of unified Germany.

Table 3.7 International Migration from and to Germany, 1984–94 (in thousands)

Year	Immigration	Emigration	Balance
Ethnic Germans, German citizens			
1984	82.2	60.3	21.9
1985	84.4	59.1	25.3
1986	90.3	59.6	30.7
1987	119.4	64.5	54.9
1988	213.0	60.5	152.5
1989	407.6	106.7	300.9
1990	460.5	109.0	351.6
1991	262.4	84.8	177.7
1992	281.8	86.7	195.2
1993	281.1	86.6	194.5
1994	296.1	119.1	177.0
1984–94	2,578.8	896.9	1,681.9
Foreigners			
1984	333.3	546.5	-213.2
1985	400.0	367.7	32.2
1986	479.5	348.0	131.5
1987	473.3	334.2	139.1
1988	648.6	359.1	289.5
1989	770.8	438.3	332.5
1990	842.4	466.0	376.3
1991	920.5	497.5	423.0
1992	1207.6	614.7	592.9
1993	986.9	710.2	276.6
1994	773.9	621.4	152.5
1984–94	7,836.8	5,303.6	2,533.2
Germans, Foreigners			
1984	415.5	606.7	-191.2
1985	484.4	426.8	57.6
1986	569.8	407.6	132.2
1987	592.8	398.7	194.0
1988	861.6	419.6	442.0
1989	1,178.3	545.0	633.4
1990	1,302.9	575.0	727.9
1991	1,182.9	582.2	600.7
1992	1,489.4	701.4	788.0
1993	1,268.0	796.9	471.1
1994	1,070.0	740.5	329.5
1984–94	10,415.6	6,200.4	4,215.2

Note: For 1984–94, Germany in its present borders; migration between East and West Germany not included in figures.

Source: Data from the Statistisches Bundesamt; Schulz 1994.

There is evidence that these high levels of immigration to Germany do not constitute a new norm but were rather a transitional phenomenon. Compared to the peak levels of 1988–1992, immigration to Germany decreased in both 1993 and 1994. In fact, immigration of ethnic Germans had already dropped in 1991. In addition, a more restrictive asylum law has been in force since 1993. Lately, legal immigration of foreigners has been on the decline, and remigration is rising: while immigration of foreigners (including asylum seekers) decreased from 1.2 million in 1992 to 774,000 in 1994, remigration increased slightly, from 615,000 in 1992 to 621,000 in 1994 (see table 3.7).

Taken together, these tendencies may help to defuse widespread fears of uncontrolled mass migration. In view of the parallel development of immigration and remigration since 1988, it can be expected that a considerable proportion of the current foreign immigrants will only stay in Germany temporarily, i.e., for a few months or years at most. This is particularly true for seasonal and contract workers as well as for most foreign students. But the same can be said of many asylum seekers who were not accepted as political refugees and for many Bosnians under temporary protection, whose status will expire in 1996/97. If these suppositions are correct, remigration will continue at a high level in the 1990s, and the positive migration balance will continue to decrease (see figure 3.11).

Future Development of the Foreign Population in Germany

At the end of 1994 Germany had 81.5 million inhabitants, of whom 7.1 million were foreigners (9 percent of the total). Since 1973 the share of foreign nationals has doubled in spite of a recruitment stop and a decrease in the amount of foreign labor between 1974 and 1985. The main reasons for this were family reunion (spouses, children), the large number of asylum seekers between 1988 and 1994, and the growing proportion of children born to foreigners in Germany (13 percent of all children born in Germany in 1994), who, according to the current citizenship law, automatically become part of the foreign population (on German citizenship law, see Gerald L. Neuman, "Nationality Law in the United States and Germany," ch. 8 in vol. 5 of this series).

Figure 3.11 Net Migration Balance for Ethnic Germans, German Citizens, and Foreigners, 1954–1995

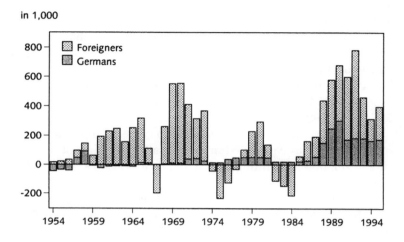

Source: Data from the Statistisches Bundesamt.

The future size of Germany's foreign population will mainly depend on three factors:

- the development of immigration and remigration of Germans and foreigners;
- the fertility of Germans and foreigners in Germany; and
- the development of the naturalization rate.

Population projections illustrate what might happen if current trends continue. The main difference will lie in the future net migration balance. From today's point of view, three different scenarios are conceivable.[18]

Scenario 1 assumes an annual net immigration of 190,000 foreigners, based on the experience of past years. This figure is the sum of net immigration streams as estimated individually for Turkey, the successor states of former Yugoslavia, the EU countries, asylum seekers (excluding those from Turkey and former Yugoslavia), and remaining countries of origin. It further assumes that the future net immigration of ethnic Germans will reach an average of 100,000 persons per year until 2000 and then decline to an annual average of 20,000 until 2015. Finally, it assumes (as do scenarios 2 and 3) an annual naturalization of 60,000 foreigners for the projection period. In the opinion of the authors, scenario 1 is the most probable case.

Scenario 2 assumes a more rigid immigration regime. Even in this case, the annual net immigration of foreigners would be around 80,000. Forced attempts to restrict future immigration would probably not leave the annual immigration of ethnic Germans untouched at its current level, and we assumed a reduction to 50,000 annually until 2010 and to 25,000 annually until 2015.

Scenario 3 illustrates the medium-range effects of an open immigration regime. Here an annual net immigration of 300,000 foreigners and 220,000 ethnic Germans has been assumed. This case is not too far from the actual migration balances from 1986 through 1994. Its prolongation over such an extended period of time (until 2030) would be quite a qualitative break, compared with Germany's migration experience of the last decades.

All three scenarios assume that the low rate of naturalization will continue.

The results of our projection show the following: In scenario 1, Germany's population (81.5 million in 1995) would decline only slightly until the year 2015 (to 80.3 million), even with moderate net immigration (more than 300,000 people per annum). After the year 2015, the aging of the population and the excess of deaths over births would increase dramatically, and the total population would decline to 74.8 million by 2030. Despite the small number of immigrants, the share of foreigners (8.8 percent in 1995) would rise to 16.9 percent of the total population by the year 2030 if naturalization rates remained as low as they are today (see table 3.8).

With a low-immigration scenario with continuing net immigration of 130,000 per year (scenario 2), the population in Germany would shrink to 77.6 million by 2015 and to 70.0 million in 2030. The aging process would be faster than in the previous scenario. In scenario 2, the percentage of foreigners in the population would rise to 11.3 percent by 2015 and to 12.5 percent in 2030 (see table 3.8).

Table 3.8 Future Growth of Foreign Population in Germany
(Three Scenarios), 1995–2030

	2015	2030
	Total population in millions (81.3 in 1995)	
Scenario 1	80.3	74.8
Scenario 2	77.6	70.0
Scenario 3	84.3	81.2
	Foreign nationals in millions (7.1 in 1995)	
Scenario 1	10.6	12.7
Scenario 2	8.8	8.7
Scenario 3	12.5	16.6
	Percentages (8.8 in 1995)	
Scenario 1	13.2	16.9
Scenario 2	11.3	12.5
Scenario 3	14.8	20.5

Source: Authors' calculations.

In the case of scenario 3, the high-immigration scenario pro-
jecting annual net immigration of 520,000, with 300,000 foreigners and 220,000 ethnic Germans, Germany's population
would increase to 84.3 million in 2015. In the following years,
however, it would decrease to 81.2 million in 2030. The share of
foreigners would reach 14.8 percent in 2015 and grow to 20.5
percent in 2030. Because of high immigration levels and low naturalization rates, the share of foreigners in Germany could thus
increase almost threefold from 1995 to 2030. Under the assumptions made for scenario 3, in thirty-three years almost a fourth
of Germany's population would consist of foreign nationals. For
many observers, this may seem unrealistic, but we have to keep
in mind that such a tripling of the share of foreigners already
occurred once before, between 1963 and 1994.

Even more remarkable is the result of scenario 2, because it
shows that even if there were a quasi-standstill in the immigration of foreigners, their share among the total population would
still almost double within the next thirty-four years. The growth
of the foreign population itself would not be the only reason for
this; the expected decline of the native German population—
attributable to the growing excess of deaths over births among

Germans and the low rate of naturalization among foreigners—also comes into play.

In all three scenarios, the impact would be most felt in large urban agglomerations. Depending on the number of immigrants in these areas, the share of foreigners would increase to more than 30 percent and could even reach 45 percent in 2030 in the ten most densely populated regions of West Germany, which already have the highest percentages of foreigners. It is hard to imagine the workings of local affairs and municipal politics in cities where one in three or one in two inhabitants had no right to vote or to be elected.

Future Prospects

In the near future, Germany will be confronted with 12 to 16 million legal residents with foreign nationality living on its territory. And even as a self-declared nonimmigrant society, the country will have to deal with a certain amount of future immigration. The large number of *Aussiedler*, labor migrants, and dependent family members who moved to Germany during the last few decades is one indicator of the enormous difference in prosperity and stability between Western Europe and most other parts of the world. Politics must face up to this reality. One of the conditions for this is the amendment of the legal and social framework for immigration and integration. Germany needs an immigration law with quota regulations, easier access to German citizenship, and more equal treatment of native Germans, ethnic German immigrants, and other legal immigrants. The two latter groups need help in integration; both should receive a fair chance of making Germany their home if they so wish. Neither of the two groups, however, can be integrated at zero cost.

Legal amendments alone will not be enough. The country also needs to change the way it perceives Germany as an ethnically defined nation-state, conferring citizenship primarily on the children of natives and on coethnics from Eastern Europe. To this day, the idea that one can only be a German if one's ancestors were German is still dominant. This popular concept reduces the chances for foreigners to integrate successfully into German society and makes any reform of the partly outdated law on citizenship more difficult. Moreover, the vision of a so-called pure ethnonation is obviously at odds with the ethnic and religious diversity that has emerged in the country since the mid-1960s. Germany badly needs a more realistic self-image as a de facto immigration country, a more relaxed approach to the diversity that has come into existence over the past decades, a greater commitment to the principle of integrating immigrants and foreigners born in the country, and an active discussion of the common principles to which Germans by birth, naturalized Germans, and foreign nationals with permanent residence in Germany should all adhere.

Notes

1. E.g., it can be found in the German national report for the International Conference on Population and Development in Cairo in 1994 and in other recent declarations by the Ministry of the Interior (Home Office).
2. In 1945 the Allies allowed Czechoslovakia and Poland to expel all German citizens and ethnic Germans living within their borders (2.9 million in Czechoslovakia, 670,000 in Poland); Poland was also permitted to expell any such individuals living in the former German territories it was now administering (6.2 million in all). At the same time, ethnic Germans were expelled by Yugoslavia (360,000), Hungary (225,000), and the USSR (1.5 million, most from the northern part of annexed East Prussia and from the Baltic republics). Parts of Romania's ethnic German minority (205,000) were sent as forced labor to the USSR and later allowed to leave for East and West Germany. See Lemberg and Edding 1959; Fassmann and Münz 1994a.
3. According to information from the Ministry of Foreign Affairs, annually some 20,000 to 25,000 Poles successfully reclaim German citizenship because they themselves or at least one of their parents were holding German citizenship during the German occupation of Poland. This reclamation is not affected by the Kriegsfolgenbereinigungsgesetz.
4. Today, the most prominent of these early West-East migrants is Lothar Bisky, the leader of the postcommunist party (PDS).
5. This sum does not include 200,000 East Germans (mostly residents of East Berlin and Brandenburg) who commute daily to workplaces in West Berlin. See also "Ost-West Pendeln" 1994.
6. This figure does not include West Germans emigrating to East Germany (see section Migration Between East and West Germany, above).

7. This figure does not include East German and ethnic immigrants to West Germany (*Übersiedler* and *Aussiedler*, respectively). These immigrants were registered on arrival by the Bundesvergleichsamt or the Bundesverwaltungsamt but only entered migration statistics after a certain delay. It would thus be inappropriate to subtract these two groups from the immigration of Germans as reported by migration statistics for individual years. For longer periods, however, this calculation gives a rough estimate of the emigration and immigration of other Germans.

8. Especially foreign laborers and expellees from the USSR were repatriated against their will, often sent to labor camps in the gulag, otherwise punished, or executed by Soviet authorities after their return. The Western allies stopped this forced repatriation only in late 1946. After that, the logic of the cold war prevailed (Fassman and Münz 1994a).

9. Armando Rodriguez, a Portuguese national, was declared to be the one-millionth guest worker. On arriving in Germany, he received an official welcome at Cologne-Deutz railway station and was offered a motorcycle. The German news magazine *Der Spiegel* devoted its cover story to this event, picturing Rodriguez on the cover (see Fassman and Münz 1994b; Münz and Ulrich 1993).

10. Since 1995, the EU has had fifteen members (Austria, Belgium, Denmark, Finland, France, Germany, Greece, Ireland, Italy, Luxembourg, the Netherlands, Portugal, Spain, Sweden, and the UK). The European Economic Area comprises the EU, Iceland, Liechtenstein, and Norway.

11. Quota refugees are not included in this sum.

12. In 1990 the last GDR government (de Maizière) had invited Soviet Jews to settle in (East) Germany in order to revive the Jewish communities in that country. This invitation was not renewed after German unification, but the arrangement still holds.

13. We can assume that this financial compensation has never reached any of the Gypsies who were persuaded or forced to return to Romania.

14. Greece, Spain, and Portugal also were not members of the EC (now the EU, i.e., European Union) at that time.

15. This freedom of settlement does not apply to nationals from other EU member countries who have no regular income or other means of subsistence. Such individuals may neither settle nor claim social welfare benefits in Germany.

16. Until 1996/97 this applied to victims of war and ethnic cleansing, especially people from Bosnia and Croatia. The status also applies to asylum seekers who were not accepted as political refugees but are not deported in the immediate term.

17. In construction, Irish and Portuguese companies hold a considerable share of the market because they are able to pay their workers and employees wages substantially below the German level. In 1996-7 several attempts were made to introduce minimum wages for the German construction industry (*Entsenderichtlinie*) that would also extend to workers from other EU countries.

18. For all three scenarios, it is assumed that the total fertility rate (TFR) of foreigners will adjust from its current level (estimated at 1.5) to 1.4 in the year 2010 and remain constant thereafter. For the complementing scenarios covering the German population, a constant TFR of 1.3 is assumed. For

foreigners' mortality, an increase in female life expectancy at birth from the current seventy-nine years to eighty years in 2030 is assumed; for men, an increase from sixty-eight to seventy-five is assumed. In a similar pattern for the German population, male and female life expectancy has been assumed to increase.

References

Arbeitsmarktanalyse für die alten und die neuen Bundesländer. 1994, 1995. Amtliche Nachrichten der Bundesanstalt für Arbeit, Sondernummer. Nuremberg: Bundesanstalt für Arbeit

Bade, Klaus J. 1994a. *Ausländer, Aussiedler, Asyl.* Munich: Beck.

_____. 1990. *Neue Heimat im Westen: Vertriebene, Flüchtlinge, Aussiedler.* Münster: Verlag Westfälischer Heimatbund.

_____, ed. 1994b. *Das Manifest der 60: Deutschland und die Einwanderung.* Munich: Beck.

_____, ed. 1992. *Deutsche im Ausland—Fremde in Deutschland: Migration in Geschichte und Gegenwart.* Munich: Beck.

Bals, Christel. 1989. "Aussiedler—Erneut ein räumliches Problem?" *Informationen zur Raumentwicklung* 4: 305–17.

Barth, Sigrun, and Winfried Hain. 1991. "Demographie und Rentenversicherung: Langfristige Vorausrechnungen zu den Rentenfinanzierungen." *Deutsche Rentenversicherung* 10–11: 724–39.

Benz, Wolfgang, ed. 1985. *Die Vertreibung der Deutschen aus dem Osten: Ursachen, Ereignisse, Folgen.* Frankfurt: Fischer.

Bericht der Beauftragten der Bundesregierung für die Belange der Ausländer über die Lage der Ausländer in der Bundesrepublik Deutschland 1995. 1995. Bonn: Mitteilungen der Beauftragten der Bundesregierung für die Belange der Ausländer.

Bethlehem, Siegfried. 1982. *Heimatvertreibung, DDR-Flucht, Gastarbeiter, Zuwanderung, Wanderungsströme und Wanderungspolitik in der Bundesrepublik Deutschland.* Stuttgart: Klett-Cotta.

BfLR. 1993. "Perspektiven der künftigen Bevölkerungsentwicklung in Deutschland." *Informationen zur Raumentwicklung* (special issues) 9/10, 11/12.

Birg, Herwig, and Ernst-Jürgen Flöthmann. 1993. *Bevölkerungsprojektionen für das wiedervereinigte Deutschland bis zum Jahr 2100*. Bielefeld: Institut für Bevölkerungsforschung und Sozialpolitik der Universität Bielefeld.

Blahusch, Friedrich. 1994. "Flüchtlinge in Deutschland nach der Asylrechtsänderung im Grundgesetz: Die Veränderung der sozialen und politischen Situation für die Bundesrepublik und die Flüchtlinge." In *Internationale Wanderungen*, ed. Rainer Münz, Hermann Korte, and Gert Wagner, 143–57. Demographie aktuell 5. Berlin: Humboldt University.

Blaschke, Dieter. 1991. "Sozialbilanz der Aussiedlung in den 80er und 90er Jahren." In *Integration von Vertriebenen*, ed. H.-P. Baumeister, 35–77. Weinheim: Beltz.

Blaschke, Jochen. 1991. "International Migration and East-West Migration: Political and Economic Paradoxes." *Migration* 11/12: 290–46.

Brubaker, William Rogers. 1992. *The Politics of Citizenship in France and Germany*. Cambridge.: Harvard University Press.

Bucher, Hansjörg, Martina Kocks, and Mathias Siedhoff. 1994. "Die künftige Bevölkerungsentwicklung der Regionen Deutschlands." *Informationen zur Raumentwicklung* 12: 501–11.

_____. 1992. "Wanderungen von Ausländern in der Bundesrepublik Deutschland der 80er Jahre." *Informationen zur Raumentwicklung* 7/8: 501–11.

Chesnais, Jean-Claude. 1991. *The USSR Emigration: Past, Present and Future*. Paris: OECD.

Chesnais, Jean-Claude. 1993. "The New Migratory Deal in Europe." In *Materialien zur Bevölkerungswissenschaft*, ed. Bundesinstitut für Bevölkerungsforschung, 79:87–100. Wiesbaden: BIB.

Cohen, Robin, ed. 1995. *The Cambridge Survey on Migration*. Cambridge: Cambridge University Press.

Cohn-Bendit, Daniel, and Thomas Schmid. 1992. *Heimat Babylon: Das Wagnis der multikulturellen Demokratie*. Hamburg: Hoffmann u. Campe.

Council of Europe. 1994. *Recent Demographic Developments in Europe*. Strasbourg: Council of Europe.

Daten und Fakten zur Ausländersituation. 1994. Bonn: Mitteilungen der Beauftragten der Bundesregierung für die Belange der Ausländer.

Delfs, Silke. 1993. "Heimatvertriebene, Aussiedler, Spätaussiedler." *Aus Politik und Zeitgeschichte: Das Parlament* B48/93: 3–11.

Dinkel, Reiner Hans, and Uwe Lebok. 1994. "Demographische Aspekte der vergangenen und zukünftigen Zuwanderung nach Deutschland." *Aus Politik und Zeitgeschichte: Das Parlament* B48/94: 27–36.

_____. 1993. "Könnten durch Zuwanderung die Alterung der Bevölkerung und die daraus resultierenden Zusatzlasten der Sozialen Sicherung aufgehalten oder gemildert werden?" *Deutsche Rentenversicherung* 6: 388–400.

Dohse, Knuth. 1981. *Ausländische Arbeitnehmer und bürgerlicher Staat*. Königstein: Hain.

Dorbritz, Jürgen. 1994. "Bericht 1994 über die demographische Lage in Deutschland." *Zeitschrift für Bevölkerungswissenschaft* 4: 398–473.

Dorbritz, Jürgen, and Karla Gärtner. 1995. "Bericht 1995 über die demographische Lage in Deutschland." *Zeitschrift für Bevölkerungswissenschaft* 4: 339–448.

Dorbritz, Jürgen, and Wulfram Speigner. 1990. "Die Deutsche Demokratische Republik: Ein Ein- und Auswanderungsland?" *Zeitschrift für Bevölkerungswissenschaft* 1: 67–86.

Das Einbürgerungs- und Staatsangehörigkeitsrecht der Bundesrepublik Deutschland. 1993. Bonn: Mitteilungen der Beauftragten der Bundesregierung für die Belange der Ausländer.

Faist, Thomas. 1994. "How to Define a Foreigner? The Symbolic Politics of Immigration in German Partisan Discourse, 1978–1992." In *The Politics of Immigration in Western Europe*, ed. Martin Baldwin-Edwards and Martin A. Schain, 50–71. Newbury-Portland: Frank Cass.

Fassman, Heinz, and Rainer Münz. 1994a. "European East-West Migration, 1945–1992." *International Migration Review* 3: 520–38.

_____, eds. 1994b. *European Migration in the Late Twentieth Century*. Aldershot: Edward Elgar.

Franz, Wolfgang. 1991. "International Migratory Movements: The German Experience." University of Konstanz, Discussion Paper Series II 160.

Frantzioch, Marion. 1987. *Die Vertriebenen: Hemmnisse, Antriebskräfte und Wege ihrer Integration in der Bundesrepublik Deutschland*. Schriften zur Kultursoziologie 9. Berlin: Dietrich Reimer Verlag.

Gesetz zur Bereinigung von Kriegsfolgensetzen vom 21. Dezember 1992 (Kriegsfolgenbereinigungsgesetz: KfbG). 1992. Promulgated in Bonn on 24 Dec. *Bundesgesetzblatt* 1, no. 58.

Gesetz zur Regelung des Aufnahmeverfahrens für Aussiedler vom 28. Juni 1990 (Aussiedleraufnahmegesetz: AAG). 1990. Promulgated in Bonn on 30 June. *Bundesgesetzblatt* 1, no. 58.

Gierse, Matthias. 1990. "Kurzfristige Arbeitsmarktwirkungen des Zustroms von Aus- und Übersiedlern." *RWI-Mitteilungen* 41: 153–67.

Globus Kartendienst. 1995. *Ausländer als Unternehmer*. Sa-2713. Hamburg: Globus Kartendienst, 6 June.

Göddecke-Stellmann, Jürgen. 1994. "Räumliche Implikationen der Zuwanderung von Aussiedlern und Ausländern: Rückkehr zu alten Mustern oder Zeitenwende?" *Informationen zur Raumentwicklung* 5/6: 373–86.

Grundmann, Siegfried. 1994. "Die Migration aus den neuen in die alten Bundesländer: Ein Spezialfall der europäischen Ost-West-Migration?" In *Internationale Wanderungen*, ed. Rainer Münz, Hermann Korte, and Gert Wagner, 41–65. Demographie aktuell 5. Berlin: Humboldt University.

Heilig, Gerhard, Thomas Büttner, and Wolfgang Lutz. 1990. *Germany's Population: Turbulent Past, Uncertain Future*. Population Bulletin 41. Washington D.C.: Population Reference Bureau.

Heitman, Sidney. 1994. "Soviet Emigration since 1985." *Nationalities Papers* 1: 247–61.

———. 1987. "The Third Soviet Emigration: Jewish, German and Armenian Emigration from the USSR since World War II." Berichte des Bundesinstituts für ostwissenschaftliche und internationale Studien, Cologne.

Herbert, Ulrich. 1986. *Geschichte der Ausländerbeschäftigung in Deutschland, 1880–1990*. Berlin-Bonn: Dietz.

Herrmann, Helga. 1992. *Ausländer: Vom Gastarbeiter zum Wirtschaftsfaktor*. Cologne: Institut der deutschen Wirtschaft.

Hof, Bernd. 1994. "Möglichkeiten und Grenzen der Eingliederung von Zuwanderern in den deutschen Arbeitsmarkt." *Aus Politik und Zeitgeschichte: Das Parlament* B48/94: 11–25.

———. 1993. *Europa im Zeichen der Migration: Szenarien zur Bevölkerungs- und Arbeitsmarktentwicklung in der Europäischen Gemeinschaft bis 2020*. Cologne: Deutscher Instituts-Verlag.

———. 1989. "Modellierung zu den Auswirkungen einer verstärkten Aussiedler-Zuwanderung auf Bevölkerung, Wirtschaftswachstum und Arbeitsmarkt." In *Die Integration deutscher Aussiedler: Perspektiven für die Bundesrepublik Deutschland*, ed. Institut der deutschen Wirtschaft, 38–72. Cologne: IW.

Hoffmann, Lutz. 1990. *Die unvollendete Republik: Zwischen Einwanderungsland und deutschen Nationalstaat*. Cologne: Papyrossa.

Hofrichter, Jürgen, and Michael Klein. 1994. "Festung Europa: Das Ausmaß der Abneigung gegenüber Immigranten in der europäischen Gemeinschaft zu Beginn der 90er Jahre." *Informationen zur Raumentwicklung* 5/6: 321–34.

Höhn, Charlotte, and Detlev B. Rein, eds. 1990. *Ausländer in der Bundesrepublik Deutschland*. Boppard: Boldt.

Höhn, Charlotte, Ulrich Mammey, and Hartmut Wendt. 1991. "Bericht 1990 zur demographischen Lage in beiden Teilen Deutschlands." *Zeitschrift für Bevölkerungswissenschaft* 2: 135–205.

Holst, Elke, and Jürgen Schupp. 1994. "Integration deutscher Zuwanderer in den westdeutschen Arbeitsmarkt." *DIW-Wochenbericht* 35: 609–17.

Hullen, Gerd, and Reiner Schulz. 1994. "Bericht 1993 zur demographischen Lage in Deutschland." *Zeitschrift für Bevölkerungswissenschaft* 1: 3–70.

Jungfer, Eberhard, Susanne Heim, Horst Kahrs, and Ahlrich Meyer. 1993. *Arbeitsmigration und Flucht: Vertreibung und Arbeitskräfteregulierung im Zwischenkriegseuropa.* Berlin: Vlg. Schwarze Risse/Rote Strasse.

Korcelli, Piotr. 1994. "Emigration from Poland after 1945." In *European Migration in the Late Twentieth Century*, ed. Heinz Fassmann and Rainer Münz, 171–86. Aldershot: Edward Elgar.

Kulischer, Eugene. 1948. *Europe on the Move: War and Population Changes, 1917–1947.* New York: Columbia University Press.

Leciejewski, Klaus. 1990. "Zur wirtschaftlichen Eingliederung der Aussiedler." *Aus Politik und Zeitgeschichte: Das Parlament* B3/90: 52–62.

Leggewie, Claus. 1990. *MultiKulti: Spielregeln für die Vielvölkerrepublik.* Berlin: Rotbuch.

Lemberg, Eugen, and Friedrich Edding, eds. 1959. *Die Vertriebenen in Deutschland.* 3 vols. Kiel: F. Hirt.

v. Loeffelholz, and Hans Dietrich. 1994. "Zuwanderung: Erfahrungen und Perspektiven der Zuwanderung in die Bundesrepublik aus ökonomischer Sicht." In *Von der Ausländer—zur Einwanderungspolitik*, ed. Forschungsinstitut der Friedrich-Ebert-Stiftung, 41–60. Bonn: Forschungsinstitut der Friedrich-Ebert-Stiftung.

Luettinger, Peter. 1986. "Der Mythos der schnellen Integration: Eine empirische Untersuchung zur Integration der Vertriebenen und Flüchtlinge in der Bundesrepublik Deutschland bis 1971." *Zeitschrift für Soziologie* 1: 20–36.

Martin, Philip. 1991. *The Unfinished Story: Turkish Labor Migration to Western Europe.* Geneva: ILO.

Mehrländer, Ursula, and Günther Schulze. 1994. "Einwanderungskonzept für die Bundesrepublik Deutschland." In *Von der Ausländer—zur Einwanderungspolitik*, ed. Forschungsinstitut der Friedrich-Ebert-Stiftung, 25–40. Bonn: Forschungsinstitut der Friedrich-Ebert-Stiftung.

Meier-Braun, Karl-Heinz, and Martin A. Kilgus, eds. 1994. *Einwanderungsland Deutschland.* Stuttgart: Süddeutscher Rundfunk.

Meis, Norbert. 1993. *Aspekte struktureller und differentieller Mobilität von Ausländern in der Bundesrepublik Deutschland.* Materialien zur Bevölkerungswissenschaft 78. Wiesbaden: Bundesinstitut für Bevölkerungswissenschaft.

Münz, Rainer, and Ralf Ulrich. 1994. "Demographische Entwicklung in Ostdeutschland und in ausgewählten Regionen: Analyse und Prognose bis 2010." *Zeitschrift für Bevölkerungswissenschaft* 4: 475–515.

_____. 1993. "Migration und Ausländerbeschäftigung in Deutschland." *StadtBauwelt* 118: 1270–72.

OECD/SOPEMI. 1994. *Trends in International Migration: Continuous Reporting System on Migration.* Annual Report 1993. Paris: OECD.

"Ost-West-Pendeln gehört zur Normalität des gesamtdeutschen Arbeitsmarktes." 1994. *DIW-Wochenbericht* 51/52: 861–66.

Reichling, Gustav. 1985. *Die deutschen Vertriebenen in Zahlen,* vol. 1, *Umsiedler, Verschleppte, Vertriebene, Aussiedler, 1940–85.* Bonn: Kulturstiftung der Vertriebenen; Meckenheim: Warlich.

Reyher, Lutz, and Hans-Uwe Bach. 1989. "Der Potential-Effekt der Zuwanderungen: Eine Arbeitskräfte-Gesamtrechnung für Aus- und Übersiedler." *Mitteilungen aus der Arbeitsmarkt- und Berufsforschung* 4: 468–71.

Ronge, Volker. 1993. "Ost-West-Wanderung nach Deutschland." *Aus Politik und Zeitgeschichte: Das Parlament* B7/93: 16–28.

Rudolph, Hedwig. 1994. "Dynamics of Immigration in a Non-Immigrant Country: Germany." In *European Migration in the Late Twentieth Century,* ed. Heinz Fassmann and Rainer Münz, 113–26. Aldershot: Edward Elgar.

Rudolph, Hedwig, and Mirjana Morokvasic, eds. 1994. *Bridging States and Markets: International Migration in the Early 1990s.* Berlin: Ed. Sigma.

Schmidt, Christoph M., and Klaus F. Zimmermann. 1992. "Migration Pressure in Germany: Past and Future." In *Migration and Economic Development,* ed. Klaus F. Zimmermann, 201–30. Berlin: Springer.

Schulz, Erika. 1994. *Zuwanderungen der letzten zehn Jahre und Abschätzung des Bestandes zum 31.12.1993.* DIW-Discussion paper 99. Berlin: Deutsches Institut für Wirtschaftsforschung.

_____. 1993. "Bevölkerungsentwicklung in Deutschland bis zum Jahr 2010 mit Ausblick auf 2040." *DIW Wochenbericht* 29: 318–25.

_____. 1991. *Die Wanderungen ins Bundesgebiet seit 1984.* DIW-Discussion paper 28. Berlin: Deutsches Institut für Wirtschaftsforschung.

_____. 1990. "Szenarien der Bevölkerungsentwicklung in der Bundesrepublik Deutschland." *DIW-Wochenbericht* 8: 93–102.

Seifert, Wolfgang. 1995. *Die Mobilität der Migranten. Die berufliche, ökonomische und soziale Stellung ausländischer Arbeitnehmer in der Bundesrepublik: Eine Längsschnittanalyse mit dem sozio-ökonomischen Panel, 1984–1989.* Berlin: Ed. Sigma.

_____. 1991. *Ausländer in der Bundesrepublik: Soziale und ökonomische Mobiität.* AG Sozialberichterstattung. Berlin: WZB.

Sprink, Joachim, and Wolfgang Hellmann. 1989. "Finanzielle Belastung oder ökonomisches Potential: Regional unterschiedliche Konsequenzen des Aussiedlerzustroms." *Informationen zur Raumentwicklung* 5: 323–29.

Stanek, Eduard. 1985. *Verfolgt—verjagt—vertrieben: Flüchtlinge in Österreich, 1945–84.* Vienna-Munich-Zurich: Europa-Verlag.

Statistisches Bundesamt. 1994a. *Datenreport 1994: Zahlen und Fakten über die Bundesrepublik Deutschland.* Bonn: Bundeszentrale für politische Bildung.

_____, ed. 1994b. *Statistisches Jahrbuch 1994 für die Bundesrepublik Deutschland.* Wiesbaden: Metzler and Poeschel.

Steinmann, Gunter, and Ralf Ulrich, eds. 1994. *The Economic Consequences of Immigration to Germany.* Heidelberg: Physica-Verlag.

Sterbling, Anton. 1994. "Die Aussiedlung der Deutschen aus Rumänien: Motive, Randbedingungen und Eigendynamik eines Migrationsprozesses." In *Internationale Wanderungen,* ed. Rainer Münz, Hermann Korte, and Gert Wagner, 66–74. Demographie aktuell 5. Berlin: Humboldt University.

Tichy, Roland. 1990. *Ausländer rein! Warum es kein "Ausländerproblem" gibt.* Munich: Piper.

Tiedtke, Klaus-Peter. 1992. "Die deutschen Aussiedler: Hintergründe, Fakten und Perspektiven der Aussiedlung und der Eingliederung." *Informationen zur Raumentwicklung* 5: 343–52.

Ulrich, Ralf. 1994. "The Future Growth of Foreign Population in Germany." In *The Economic Consequences of Immigration to Germany,* ed. Gunter Steinmann and Ralf Ulrich, 21–44. Heidelberg: Physica-Verlag.

_____. 1990. *Migration to the Federal Republic and the End of the GDR.* FIB Papers P 90-302, Publication Series of the International Relations Resarch Group. Berlin: WZB.

Velling, Johannes. 1994. *Zuwanderer auf dem Arbeitsmarkt: Sind die neuen Migranten die "Gastarbeiter" der neunziger Jahre?* ZEW-Wirtschaftsanalysen 3. Mannheim: ZEW.

_____. 1993a. *Immigration to Germany in the Seventies and Eighties: The Role of Family Reunification.* ZEW Discussion Paper 93-18. Mannheim: ZEW.

_____. 1993b. *Schengen, Dublin und Maastricht: Etappen auf dem Weg zu einer europäischen Immigrationspolitik.* ZEW Discussion Paper No. 93-11. Mannheim: ZEW.

Velling, Johannes, and Malte Woydt. 1993. *Migrationspolitiken in ausgewählten Industriestaaten: Ein synoptischer Vergleich Deutschland—Frankreich—Italien—Spanien—Kanada.* ZEW Documentation. Mannheim: ZEW.

Wendt, Hartmut. 1994. "Wanderungen nach und innerhalb von Deutschland unter besonderer Berücksichtigung der Ost-West Wanderungen." *Zeitschrift für Bevölkerungswissenschaft* 4: 517–40.

Werner, Heinz. 1993. *Integration ausländischer Arbeitnehmer in den Arbeitsmarkt: Deutschland, Frankreich, Niederlande, Schweden.* World Employment Programme, Working Paper MIG WP.74 D. Geneva: ILO.

Werner, Heinz, and Wolfgang Seifert. 1994. *Die Integration ausländischer Arbeitnehmer in den Arbeitsmarkt.* Beiträge zur Arbeitsmarkt- und Berufsforschung 178. Nuremberg: Institut für Arbeitsmarkt- und Berufsforschung der Bundesanstalt für Arbeit.

Wiegand, Erich. 1992. *Zunahme der Ausländerfeindlichkeit? Einstellung zu Fremden in Deutschland und Europa.* ZUMA-Nachrichten 31. N.p.

_____. 1984. *Die Inanspruchnahme ausgewählter Sozialleistungen durch Ausländer: Ergebnisse der Ausländerumfrage 1982.* SFB 3 working paper 134. Frankfurt-Mannheim: SFB 3.

Winkler, Beate. 1994. "Einwanderung: Kernfrage unserer Gesellschaft und Herausforderung an die Politik." *Aus Politik und Zeitgeschichte: Das Parlament* B 48/94: 3–9.

_____, ed. 1992. *Zukunftsangst Einwanderung.* Munich: Beck.

Chapter 4

The Changing Demography of U.S. Immigration Flows
Patterns, Projections, and Contexts*

Frank D. Bean, Robert G. Cushing,
and Charles W. Haynes

Immigration issues have risen once again to a prominent place on the public policy agenda of the United States (Fix and Passel 1994; Teitelbaum and Weiner 1995; U.S. Commission on Immigration Reform 1994). Concomitantly, the results of public opinion polls have shown growing proportions of people who think current U.S. immigration levels are too high (Espenshade and Calhoun 1993; Bean 1993). To understand why policymakers and the public have become increasingly concerned about immigration, it is necessary first to examine recent trends in the magnitude of flows of people coming into the country compared to those at earlier time periods. Beyond this, it is also necessary to inquire into the texture of these flows, because increasing anxiety about immigration may less reflect worries about the size of flows than concerns about their national origin, socioeconomic station, and racial/ethnic composition. The relatively diminished economic prospects facing U.S. workers in recent years may also

---

* Thanks are expressed to Jennifer Van Hook, Molly Martin, and Karen Wilkinson for research and other assistance. The support of the Hewlett Foundation, the Mellon Foundation, and the Tomás Rivera Center is gratefully acknowledged.

contribute to growing doubts about immigration. The purpose of this paper is to develop a portrait of the recent major migration flows to the United States, their implications for future population composition, and their social and economic contexts, in order to shed light on why immigration has once again become an important public policy issue in the United States.

The paper is divided into four sections. The first describes the major flows of people coming into the United States during the twentieth century, especially since the end of World War II, and the changes these flows imply for racial/ethnic composition. The second examines the implications of these flows for the current and future racial/ethnic composition of the U.S. population and discusses the implications of changing patterns of interracial and interethnic marriage and racial/ethnic identification both for measuring and for interpreting the effects of changing racial/ethnic composition. The third assesses the demographic and economic contexts within which these flows have occurred. The fourth argues that a combined view of trends in migration flows, racial/ethnic composition, interracial and interethnic marriage patterns, and economic and labor market outcomes makes it possible to discern not only why recent immigration patterns have come to be negatively perceived but also why they may have come to be seen as violating the prevailing sense of social contract in the United States.

Major Flows into the United States

The major features of post-World War II migration flows to the United States include rising numbers of legal immigrants, growing numbers of refugees and asylees, mounting levels of undocumented migrants, and enormously increasing numbers of people admitted for short periods of time on so-called nonimmigrant visas. In the case of each of these categories of flows, the share of people from Hispanic and Asian countries has risen and has come to constitute a majority of the flow, while the share from European countries has been falling. This pattern has occurred at the same time that economic growth has slowed in the United States and wages have stagnated. Thus recent concerns about levels of immigration may reflect either anxieties about change in the sizes of racial/ethnic groups or worries about economic competition and job opportunities. Below we develop a portrait of recent changes in the varieties of migration flows to the United States and assess the changes in the social, demographic, and economic contexts in which they have occurred, in an attempt to shed light on the question of which are the most important sets of forces driving current reactions to U.S. immigration trends and policies.

Legal Immigrants

A number of studies have been undertaken of the changes in immigration trends and policies in the United States during the twentieth century (e.g., Bean, Vernez, and Keely 1989; Cafferty et al. 1983; Reimers 1985). All emphasize that the annual numbers of new entrants reached their highest totals during the first two decades of the century. Then, owing to the passage of the National Origins Quota Act in 1924, the Great Depression during the 1930s, and an unfavorable immigration climate during World War II, immigration numbers dropped tenfold during the next twenty-five years. Specifically, the number of entrants decreased from over seven hundred thousand per year during the first twenty years of the century to less than seventy thousand per year from 1925 through 1945 (U.S. Immigration and Naturalization Service 1995). After this lull and continuing for nearly fifty years now, legal immigration again moved steadily upward, reaching by the late 1980s and early 1990s levels approaching the all-time highs set in the early part of the twentieth century (see figure 4.1). And if the legalizations resulting from the 1986 Immigration Reform and Control Act (IRCA) are included in the totals, the recent levels exceed all previous records (U.S. Immigration and Naturalization Service 1995).

The results shown in figure 4.2 dramatically reveal the changing national origins of U.S. immigrants. Prior to 1960 the vast majority came from European countries or Canada (often over 90 percent, when examined on a decade basis). Even as late as the 1950s, just over two-thirds (67.7 percent) of all arrivals were from these countries. Things changed rapidly during the 1960s, when family reunification criteria rather than national origins quotas became the basis for granting entry visas (Bean, Vernez,

Figure 4.1 Average Number of Immigrants and Percentage of Foreign-Born

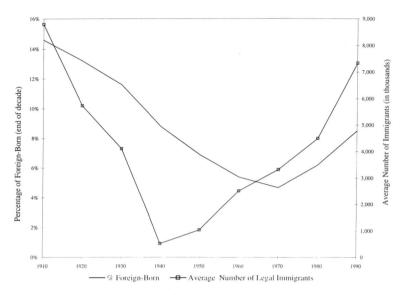

and Keely 1989; Reimers 1983). During the 1980s only 12.5 percent of legal immigrants came from Europe or Canada, whereas 84.4 percent were from Asian or Latin American countries (U.S. Immigration and Naturalization Service 1995). From 1992 to 1994, because of the provisions of Immigration Act of 1990 and the increasing numbers of immigrants from the former Soviet Union, these percentages changed to 20.6 percent from Europe and Canada and 75.9 percent from Asia and Latin America (U.S. Immigration and Naturalization Service 1995). These relatively recent changes in the national origins of immigrants have begun to convert the United States from a largely biracial society consisting of a sizable white majority and a small black minority, with a very small Native American minority of less than 1 percent, into a multiracial, multiethnic society consisting of several racial/ethnic groups (Passel and Edmonston 1994). This trend became discernible in the 1950s but began to accelerate in the 1960s (see table 4.1). By 1990 nearly a quarter of the U.S. population designated itself as either black, Hispanic, Asian, or Native American. And the growth of other groups has meant that the

Figure 4.2 Average Annual Number of Immigrants Admitted
to the United States by National Origin

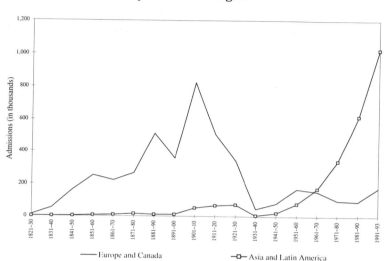

proportion of blacks in the minority population has been declining. In fact, by 1990 blacks no longer constituted a majority of
the minority population (Passel and Edmonston 1994).

Refugees and Asylees

The United States, like most other Western democracies, did not
move to incorporate explicit specifications regarding the treatment of refugees into its official immigration policy until after
World War II, when it recognized victims of political persecution
as "a distinct category of international migrants to whom [it]
owed special obligations" (Zohlberg 1992, 55). In 1948 Congress
passed the Displaced Persons Act, which was signed the month
the Berlin blockade began in Germany, permitting the entry into
the United States of 205,000 of the hundreds of thousands of
displaced persons flooding into the U.S.-occupied zones of
Europe. The drafters of the law tried to connect the legislation's
refugee resettlement provisions with U.S. immigration policy by
stipulating that the number of refugees had to be charged
against the immigration quotas of future years. In the ensuing
years, the issue of what to do about refugees continued to arise

Table 4.1 U.S. Population by Race/Ancestry, 1900–1990
(in thousands)

Year	Total	Non-Hispanic White	Black	Hispanic	Asian	American Indian
Population						
1900	76,195	66,225	8,834	656	243	237
1910	93,879	82,049	10,255	999	299	277
1920	110,747	96,969	11,512	1,632	389	244
1930	127,585	111,543	12,736	2,435	527	343
1940	136,928	119,425	13,767	2,814	577	345
1950	155,156	134,351	156,668	4,039	739	357
1960	182,055	154,969	19,071	6,346	1,146	524
1970	205,567	170,371	23,005	9,616	1,782	793
1980	226,625	180,392	26,482	14,604	3,726	1,420
1990	248,712	187,139	29,986	22,354	7,274	1,959
Percentage						
1900	100.00	86.9	11.6	0.9	0.3	0.3
1910	100.00	87.4	10.9	1.1	0.3	0.3
1920	100.00	87.6	10.4	1.5	0.4	0.2
1930	100.00	87.4	10.0	1.9	0.4	0.3
1940	100.00	87.2	10.1	2.1	0.4	0.3
1950	100.00	86.6	10.1	2.6	0.5	0.2
1960	100.00	85.1	10.5	3.5	0.6	0.3
1970	100.00	82.9	11.2	4.7	0.9	0.4
1980	100.00	79.6	11.7	6.4	1.6	0.6
1990	100.00	75.2	12.1	9.0	2.9	0.8

Note: Populations include the fifty states and the District of Columbia for 1900–1990.

Source: Adapted from table 2.3 in Passel and Edmonston 1994.

but was viewed as conflicting with other features of U.S. immigration policy, particularly the national origins quotas that severely restricted admissions from some countries. As a result of this dilemma and because it was largely driven by foreign policy considerations, U.S. refugee policy essentially had to be crafted and implemented on an ad hoc basis.

Whatever the vagaries of postwar refugee policy, the effects of the numerous ad hoc admissions programs introduced another source of new entrants into the United States. Since the end of World War II, nearly three million refugees and asylees have been granted lawful permanent resident status by the United States (U.S. Immigration and Naturalization Service 1995).

During the 1940s and 1950s the number of refugees and asylees averaged about fifty thousand per year, a figure that declined to about twenty thousand per year during the 1960s before rising to over fifty thousand per year during the 1970s, to about a hundred thousand per year during the 1980s, and to well over that number in the 1990s (see figure 4.3). As with legal immigrants, the vast majority come from Asia, Latin America, and the Caribbean (49.2 percent overall since 1945, and 82.2 percent during the 1980s), although both the relative and absolute numbers coming from the former Soviet Union have increased substantially since 1990. In sum, as figure 4.3 shows, the category of refugee and asylee admissions has constituted an increasing flow of persons into the country, predominantly Asian and Latino, over the past fifty years.

Illegal Immigrants

People who enter the United States illegally and those who enter legally and then remain illegally constitute another major flow into the country. The former are called "EWIs" by the U.S. Immigration and Naturalization Service (or simply "undocumented migrants" by other observers), because they "enter without inspection"; the latter are called "visa overstayers," because they stay beyond the expiration dates on their visas. Almost all undocumented migrants enter at the U.S.-Mexican border, with the vast majority originating in Mexico, although in recent years substantial numbers have also come from Central American countries (Bean, Edmonston, and Passel 1990). The visa overstayers do not come from any one country predominantly.

The bracero program, which started in 1942, at the beginning of World War II, provided a means whereby temporary contract laborers from Mexico could enter and work in the country legally (Calavita 1992). After the program ended in 1964, the flow of undocumented migrants into the country began to increase. That the flows of such people has become substantial is reflected in figure 4.4, which shows by decade the average number of apprehensions annually by the U.S. Border Patrol (mostly at the U.S.-Mexican border) of people illegally resident in the United States (U.S. Immigration and Naturalization Service 1995). While it is well known that such apprehensions data can-

Figure 4.3 Refugees and Asylees Granted Lawful Permanent Resident Status by National Origins (1946–1993)

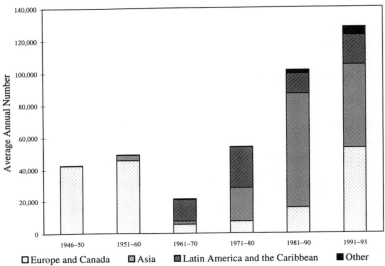

□ Europe and Canada　▨ Asia　▨ Latin America and the Caribbean　■ Other

not readily be interpreted as indicating the number of persons who illegally reside in the country and that they represent flows (the number coming in over a period of time) better than stocks (the number present at a single moment in time) and refer to events not people (Bean, Edmonston, and Passel 1990), there is little doubt that the rising numbers of apprehensions reflect increases in the number of undocumented migrants entering the country (Espenshade 1995). The stock of undocumented migrants, together with the stock of people illegally residing in the country by overstaying their visa, started to grow in the 1960s and increased substantially in the 1970s. That this number has become considerable is indicated by the U.S. Bureau of the Census's inclusion of an annual net gain of two hundred thousand illegal immigrants in its annual population estimates and projections (Campbell 1994). Other sources estimate the size of this net component to be currently in the range of two to three hundred thousand (Warren 1992).

Obviously the racial/ethnic composition of illegal immigrants is not known with the same degree of certainty as that of legal immigrants, but the available evidence suggests that the group, like

Figure 4.4 Average Annual Number of Apprehensions, 1911–1994 (by decade)

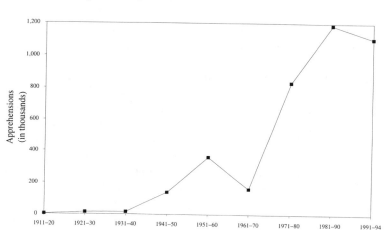

contemporary legal immigrants in general, is mainly Asian and Latin American in origin (Warren and Passel 1987; Warren 1992, 1990). This would suggest that the effect of illegal immigration on racial/ethnic composition is not greatly different from that of legal immigration, a conclusion corroborated by the national origin composition of the people who became legal immigrants under the provisions of IRCA, nearly 69.9 percent of whom were of Mexican origin and 92.4 percent of whom were of either Latin American or Asian origin (U.S. Department of Justice 1992).

Nonimmigrant Entrants

Nonimmigrants are persons admitted to the United States for a specified temporary period of time but not for permanent residence. Although the majority of nonimmigrants are tourists, large numbers of students and people coming for various business- and work-related reasons are also admitted. In fact, the numbers of people coming for business-related reasons have increased substantially in the past two or three years, an outcome facilitated by the Immigration Act of 1990, which included compromise provisions allowing easier nonimmigrant business entry in lieu of the even higher levels of employment-related immigration that some proponents wanted to include in the legislation (Bean and Fix 1992). During fiscal year 1993, 21.4 million nonimmigrant admissions to the United States were recorded, the largest number ever and an increase of 650,000 (3.1 percent) over fiscal year 1992 (U.S. Immigration and Naturalization Service 1995, 94).

Nonimmigrant admissions are an important source of flows into the country and hold significant implications for immigration issues that go beyond sheer magnitude. The dramatic increase in nonimmigrant admissions in recent years reflects the mounting demand both for tourism and for business- and employment-related entry resulting from the increased globalization of the economy. Nonimmigrant flows constitute the source from which visa overstayers develop, the group that in recent years has been estimated to make up half the illegal population in the United States at any one point in time (Warren 1990, 1992; Goodman 1995). The picture that emerges from numerous ethnographic studies of migration implies that the nonimmigrant entrants who become illegal migrants through visa overstaying do so through a social process that in turn results in many eventually becoming permanent (and often legal) immigrants (Massey et al. 1987). Hence, as the volume of nonimmigrant admissions continues to climb steeply, pressures on the legal immigration system are likely to increase, even if the rate of visa overstaying remains constant.

In addition to the fact that nonimmigrant entrants make up the pool from which visa overstayers emerge, the number and racial/ethnic composition of people in the United States on nonimmigrant visas are also likely to affect public perceptions about immigration. The average citizen seems rarely to distinguish among different kinds of immigrants, let alone among different kinds of nonimmigrants or between nonimmigrants and immigrants (Bean, Telles, and Lowell 1987). The number of nonimmigrant entrants has steadily increased over the past decade, and though the national origins of these flows have been somewhat more diverse than is the case for other kinds of flows (see figure 4.5), the proportion of nonimmigrant entrants from Asia, Latin America, and the Caribbean has grown, from about 41 percent in 1965 to about 54 percent in 1993. These rapidly rising numbers undoubtedly contribute to the impression that Latino and Asian immigration to the United States is higher than it actually is.

Figure 4.5 Annual Number of Nonimmigrants Admitted to
the United States (fiscal years 1946–1993)

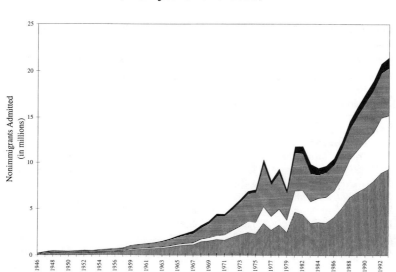

IIII Europe and Canada   ☐ Asia   ☰ Latin America and the Caribbean   ■ Other

Immigration and Current and Future Racial/Ethnic Composition

Because concerns about immigration may be rooted in fears
about the country's changing racial/ethnic composition and the
role that immigration plays in contributing to that process, it is
important to examine more precisely the contribution of immigration per se to population growth and changing population
composition. Table 4.2 shows the contribution of immigration
since 1900 to population growth (as opposed to growth resulting
from an excess of births over deaths among pre-1900 natives) for
the major racial/ethnic groups in 1990. Although post-1990
immigration has accounted for about 30 percent of the growth of
the total U.S. population since 1900, its contribution to the
growth of the various major racial/ethnic subgroups varies enormously, accounting for nearly all of the growth among Asians
and Hispanics (85.7 and 97.3 percent, respectively) and virtually
none of the growth among blacks.

Table 4.2 Contribution of Post-1900 Immigration and 1990 Population for the Population of the United States in 1990 by Race/Ethnicity (in thousands)

Contribution from Component	Total	Non-Hispanic White	Black	Hispanic	Asian
Estimated Population	248,712	187,139	29,986	22,354	7,274
1900 Population	174,145	141,369	27,493	3,108	216
1st Generation	8,534	8,184	29	301	20
2d Generation	35,574	34,118	392	956	108
3d Generation	38,547	36,735	941	869	2
4th+ Generations	90,055	60,868	26,151	991	85
immigration since 1900	74,567	45,769	2,493	19,246	7,058
1900–1910 Immigrants	17,286	16,398	125	606	157
1910–1920 Immigrants	14,487	12,624	196	1,257	409
1920–1930 Immigrants	9,305	6,661	167	2,182	295
1930–1940 Immigrants	1,439	1,021	22	312	83
1940–1950 Immigrants	3,590	2,389	68	1,055	77
1950–1960 Immigrants	5,272	2,870	158	1,885	359
1960–1970 Immigrants	5,214	1,930	266	2,433	584
1970–1980 Immigrants	9,518	2,658	834	4,013	2,014
1980–1990 Immigrants	10,756	1,341	774	5,525	3,116

Source: Adapted from table 2.4 of Passel and Edmonston 1994.

Given that immigration has recently affected U.S. racial/ethnic composition, what will the racial/ethnic composition of the U.S. population look like in the future if current immigration and other demographic trends continue? One answer is provided by population projections undertaken by the U.S. Bureau of the Census (Campbell 1994). These projections, shown in table 4.3, are based on what the bureau thinks are the most reasonable assumptions about extrapolations of current demographic trends. Although the bureau projects the Hispanic and non-Hispanic populations separately (because Hispanics may be of any race, although almost all are white), we subtract the Hispanic numbers from the numbers for non-Hispanic whites so that the totals for these two groups will be mutually exclusive. Expressed as a percentage of the total population, the four largest racial/ethnic minority groups are projected to increase from 24.8 percent of the total population in 1990 to 37.5 percent in 2020, with almost all of that increase occurring among Hispanics and Asians. Thus, given current trends (including immigration), the size of the U.S. minority population will grow considerably in just thirty years.

Table 4.3 U.S. Census Bureau Projections of Racial/Ethnic Composition of the U.S. Population (in thousands)

Year	Total	Non-Hispanic White	Black	Hispanic	Asian	American Indian
Population						
1990	248,712	187,139	29,986	22,354	7,274	1,959
2000	276,241	195,101	35,469	31,166	12,125	2,379
2010	300,431	199,772	40,224	40,525	17,191	2,719
2020	325,942	203,574	45,408	51,217	22,653	3,090
Percentages						
1900	100.0	75.2	12.1	9.0	2.9	0.8
2000	100.0	70.6	12.8	11.3	4.4	0.9
2010	100.0	66.5	13.4	13.5	5.7	0.9
2020	100.0	62.5	13.9	15.7	7.0	0.9

Source: Adapted from Campbell 1994.

The prospect of a more racially and ethnically diverse population in the future is often evoked in somewhat alarmist tones, as if such a future must necessarily lead to increased interracial and interethnic competition for jobs, housing, and social services, if not more overt conflict (Bouvier 1991; Brimelow 1995; Goodman 1995). To the extent that such scenarios of greater tension and competition are plausible, it is not difficult to imagine that the recent preponderance of Asians and Hispanics in U.S. immigration flows might generate concern about the changing racial/ethnic composition of the U.S. population and contributed to growing anti-immigrant sentiment. But how likely are such scenarios? Apart from their assumptions about demographic processes, projections about the future racial/ethnic composition of the U.S. population depend on two other critical assumptions: that racial/ethnic categories are immutable and that interracial and interethnic marriage patterns have little effect on racial/ethnic identification or on projections of future racial/ethnic composition. Neither of these assumptions seems totally warranted.

Exogamy affects estimates of the future racial/ethnic composition of the United States directly through its influence on fer-

tility, mortality, migration, and other factors that shape racial/
ethnic composition and indirectly through its impact on racial/
ethnic identification. Measuring racial/ethnic identification is
always complex, and special problems may arise in the case of
mixed-ancestry individuals whenever patterns of endogamy/
exogamy vary substantially among racial/ethnic groups and by
age and sex cohorts. In 1970 the U.S. Census changed its procedures for data collection, replacing face-to-face interviews with
self-enumeration schedules, resulting in the use of self-identification questions as the basis for measuring racial/ethnic status,
a practice that has been followed ever since. Because the factors
that influence self-identification of racial/ethnic status are not
yet well understood, particularly for people with multiple ances-
tries (Waters 1990), self-identification of ancestral roots presents
a problem in any attempt to project racial/ethnic populations
(Edmonston, Lee, and Passel 1994, 9).

Table 4.4 was extracted in part from several tables in Lieberson and Waters (1988) and calculated in part from data from the
Public Use Microdata Samples from the 1990 U.S. Census (U.S.
Bureau of the Census 1992). It illustrates that exogamy varies
among different racial/ethnic categories and has been increasing
over time. Because of the large differences in the size of different
racial/ethnic groups, inmarriage or intermarriage rates alone
can sometimes be misleading indicators of endogamy/exogamy.
The ancestry categories in table 4.4 are ordered by odds ratios
(columns 2 and 3) rather than endogamy rates (column 4). In
effect, the odds ratio contrasts the odds of a woman in a given
ancestry category having a husband with the same ancestry to
the odds of a woman outside the ancestry group having a husband from the given ancestry group. Comparing the odds ratios
for 1980 and 1990 shows that the likelihood of in-group marriage declined appreciably over time; conversely, intermarriage
increased substantially. The percentage of endogamous marriages by age cohort gives another indication of trends over time
for each racial/ethnic group (table 4.4, columns 5–10). In general, there is a lower in-group marriage rate among the younger
age cohorts for most groups, also suggesting that exogamy is
increasing over time among racial/ethnic groups. This conclusion is buttressed by National Center for Health Statistics intermarriage data on black and whites in the United States reported

by Kalmijn (1993) and Berg (1995). Both of these authors report that the incidence of black-white marriages increased more than five times within twenty years, from 1.6 percent of all marriages involving African-Americans in 1968 to 8.9 percent in 1988. Intermarriage rates between blacks and other groups and between whites and other groups have also been increasing (Berg 1995; Hacker 1995).

While increasing rates of intermarriage among racial/ethnic groups in the United States provide evidence of a more favorable climate of opinion regarding intergroup relations, it must also be kept in mind that statistics like those cited above may mostly reflect the changing behavior of people of higher socioeconomic status. People of lower socioeconomic status of all races and ethnicities in the United States have shown lower marriage rates in recent years than other groups' (McLanahan and Casper 1995). Thus any greater tolerance of intermarriage may primarily indicate greater tolerance of intermarriage among individuals of higher socioeconomic status. Even if this were the case, the near-universality of the increasing exogamy patterns across all racial/ethnic groups is impressive and undoubtedly indicates a rise in the tendency to outgroup marriage, thus blurring further the sharpness of boundaries between groups.

U.S. immigration laws have some effect on endogamy/exogamy and the racial/ethnic distribution of the population. In 1986 nearly 32 percent (approximately 125,000 individuals) of adults granted permanent resident status in the United States entered the country as the spouses or fiancé(e)s of U.S. citizens, compared to 17 and 26 percent in 1969 and 1979, respectively (Jasso and Rosenzweig 1990, 154). Current laws also favor parents, siblings, and adult offspring of U.S. citizens and residents for immigration visas. Many of those so favored by current immigration laws are adults by definition, if not already married by definition, which would lead to higher endogamy rates than would be expected for single people entering the country based on skills criteria, for example, and without the advantage of family-reunion status.

Population projections by race/ethnicity that assume unchanging racial/ethnic boundaries and patterns of identification, along with low and unchanging levels of exogamy, are likely to generate unrealistic numbers. The conventional approach to projec-

Table 4.4 Endogamy Odds for Selected Racial/Ethnic Groups, United States, 1980 and 1990

Wife's Ancestry	Odds Ratio 1980	1990	Percentage of Wives with Husbands of Same Ancestry, 1990 Total	<25	25–34	35–44	45–54	55–64	65+
English	7.7	6.2	42.3	37.0	32.5	36.5	40.7	43.4	45.3
German	4.6	4.1	48.0	45.8	44.3	43.8	47.4	49.2	52.6
Irish	4.5	4.0	37.7	30.2	31.6	31.4	35.8	40.2	39.3
French	6.0	5.6	16.4	14.0	16.2	16.7	17.9	21.4	20.9
Italian	19.0	13.8	36.5	22.9	29.1	33.2	45.9	56.2	70.3
Scottish	6.0	5.8	21.5	17.4	15.6	15.8	20.9	21.9	25.3
Polish	15.5	10.9	25.2	16.5	19.1	26.1	30.5	44.9	53.6
Dutch	9.5	9.7	18.6	17.8	16.3	12.7	18.2	25.1	27.7
Swedish	8.1	6.6	10.8	7.9	8.5	9.6	13.4	12.5	22.3
Norwegian	20.9	16.7	18.0	9.6	14.9	17.1	18.7	27.0	37.4
Russian	61.4	47.3	38.4	36.0	33.8	10.0	41.2	50.3	50.7
Czech	26.8	26.0	15.5	8.7	8.9	13.9	19.4	31.6	40.5
Hungarian	18.9	25.6	13.4	18.9	8.9	16.0	20.3	31.5	39.1
Welsh	8.4	6.3	6.5	9.3	6.1	6.1	6.2	6.4	6.7
Danish	14.2	15.9	10.1	2.1	11.8	9.0	8.7	12.4	16.3
Portuguese	180.3	200.3	37.6	43.5	47.5	47.0	57.0	63.2	56.8
Black	32,998.0	9,327.9	97.4	94.5	96.3	97.5	98.3	99.3	99.2
Mexican	742.7	458.7	79.2	81.4	76.9	76.8	81.3	84.4	88.1
Mexican, U.S. Born	732.8	316.3	69.7	71.7	65.7	67.3	75.2	81.7	86.1
Puerto Rican	3,468.0	793.7	61.4	52.6	54.2	60.0	66.2	72.6	75.4
Other Spanish	174.6	165.7	57.8	54.4	52.7	56.1	62.8	63.6	65.5
American Indian	16.4	14.5	27.9	34.5	34.2	33.0	33.5	32.7	35.6
Asian	1,178.7	730.6	72.2	59.5	70.3	71.5	76.2	75.5	89.5
Asian, U.S. Born	1,075.6	425.5	58.3	32.4	49.8	57.1	68.3	84.0	88.9
American	365.4	255.1	75.6	62.2	62.3	66.6	71.2	70.6	69.6

Note: The odds ratio contrasts the odds of a woman having a husband with the same ancestry to the odds of other women having a husband of that ancestry. The ratio takes into account the differences among ancestry groups in both in-marriage rates and the relatives sizes of the groups.

Sources: Lieberson and Waters 1988, table 6.1, based on 1980 U.S. Census Public Use Microdata Sample (couples for whom the wife is in her first marriage); 1990 U.S. Census Public Use Microdata Sample (all currently married couples) (U.S. Bureau of the Census 1992).

tions of racial/ethnic population is to assume exogamy is nonexistent by assuming single-ancestry offspring, usually taking the father's racial/ethnic status as the marker. While we know of no attempts to estimate the effects on population projections of changing patterns of racial/ethnic identification, Edmonston, Lee, and Passel (1994) have examined the potential impact of exogamy on projections of the future population of the United States by race and ethnicity. They used a modified cohort component analysis to undertake a simulation of expected populations of Asians, blacks, Hispanics, and non-Hispanic whites when differential exogamy rates are included in the estimates. They assume out-marriage rates (overall) of 0.20 for Asians, 0.03 for blacks, 0.30 for Hispanics, and 0.08 for whites (13–14). Increases in exogamy rates are built into the model for each successive generation except among whites. The expected numbers of single and mixed-ancestry people are reported in table 4.5 for each of the four groups for the next five census years. The baseline data (the fourth row in each racial/ethnic subcategory) represent the projections estimated from standard approaches to predicting population trends (i.e., assuming no exogamy and/or only single-ancestry offspring from mixed marriages).

According to the simulation, by 2040, 31.4 million or about 8.8 percent of the population, would be of mixed ancestry (28). The maximum effect on the percentage of the total population that would be minority would thus be about nine percentage points. That is, by 2040, the minority population would be 35 to 44 percent of the U.S. population depending on self-identification and on how mixed-ancestry persons identified themselves in the census.

Of the three racial/ethnic groups, the estimates for Hispanics would be most affected. Under the restrictions of the model, the Hispanic total would fall between 50.9 million and 77.4 million people by 2040, depending on the degree to which mixed ancestry people identified themselves as Hispanics (see table 4.5). Roughly two-thirds of the total would be single-ancestry Hispanics, and one-third would be mixed-ancestry Hispanics. The Asian population estimates would vary by as much as 8.5 million by 2040. The simulation suggests that the estimates for blacks would vary by only 2 million, although it should be noted that the model's exogamy assumptions for this group are

Table 4.5 Estimated U.S. Population by Ethnic Group and Single and Mixed Ancestry (1990–2040) (in millions)

Population Group	1990	2000	2010	2020	2030	2040
Total Population						
Single	248.7	272.3	290.6	306.0	317.7	324.0
Mixed	0.0	4.4	8.9	14.5	22.3	31.4
Overall	248.7	276.7	299.5	320.5	340.1	355.4
Baseline	248.7	276.7	299.5	320.5	340.1	355.4
Percentage of total	100.0	100.0	100.0	100.0	100.0	100.0
Asian						
Single	7.3	11.6	16.2	20.9	25.7	30.3
Mixed	0.0	0.8	1.9	3.4	5.6	8.5
Overall	7.3	12.4	18.1	24.4	31.3	38.7
Baseline	7.3	12.0	17.1	22.7	28.5	34.5
Percentage of total	2.9	4.3	5.7	7.1	8.4	9.7
Black						
Single	30.0	33.9	37.1	39.7	41.8	43.1
Mixed	0.0	0.3	0.6	0.9	1.4	2.0
Overall	30.0	34.2	37.7	40.6	43.2	45.1
Baseline	30.0	34.1	37.4	40.2	42.5	44.1
Percentage of total	12.1	12.3	12.5	12.5	12.5	12.4
Hispanic						
Single	22.4	28.6	35.0	41.1	46.5	50.9
Mixed	0.0	3.3	7.1	11.9	18.5	26.5
Overall	22.4	31.9	42.1	53.0	65.0	77.4
Baseline	22.4	30.3	38.6	47.1	55.7	64.2
Percentage of total	9.0	10.9	12.9	14.7	16.4	18.1
White						
Single	187.1	196.2	200.1	202.1	201.6	197.4
Mixed	0.0	4.4	8.2	12.6	19.1	26.0
Overall	187.1	200.6	208.4	214.7	220.6	223.5
Baseline	187.1	198.4	204.2	208.4	211.1	210.5
Percentage of total	75.2	71.7	68.2	65.0	62.1	59.2

Note: "Single" = population including births to parents of the same race/ethnic group; "Mixed" = population including births to parents of a different race/ethnic group; "Overall" = the total population, including single plus mixed births; "Baseline" = the total population assuming no exogamy; "Percentage of the total" = the proportion of the total population, using baseline data.

Source: Edmonston, Lee, and Passel 1994, table 5.

extremely conservative. If all mixed-ancestry people were classified as single ancestry and if they were all assumed to fall in the white total, the white, non-Hispanic population could be more than 31 million people (or nearly 15 percent) more than baseline projections by the year 2040. The actual number surfacing in census and population surveys, of course, would depend on how mixed-ancestry individuals self-identify and report their racial/ethnic status.

The Demographic and Economic Contexts

As the above trends make clear, the substantial rise in immigration occurring since World War II has consisted of several different kinds of flows and is beginning to change the country's racial/ethnic composition. The increases in each of the flows may be seen as rooted to some extent in conditions that emerged out of the postwar economic expansion. From the end of World War II to the early 1970s, the United States experienced rising economic prosperity and increasing affluence. Levels of productivity were high, and wages and personal incomes rose (Landau 1988; Levy 1987). Not by coincidence, in 1965 the country eliminated the restrictive and discriminatory national origins criteria for the admission of immigrants that were embodied in the 1924 National Origins Quota Act and ratified in the 1952 McCarran-Walter Act. Adopted in their place were more inclusionary family reunification criteria reflecting the era's domestic policy emphases on improving civil rights and foreign policy emphases on establishing better relations with newly independent third world countries (Cafferty et al. 1983). As a result of such policies in general and the family reunification provisions in particular, legal immigration began to rise substantially (Reimers 1983, 1985). At about the same time, because of the termination of the bracero program in 1964 and the growing demand for inexpensive labor, undocumented (mostly Mexican) immigration began to increase (Massey 1981). Unlike the so-called old immigrants, who were mostly European in origin, the so-called new immigrants (both legal and undocumented) came mostly from third world Hispanic and Asian countries (Bean and Tienda 1987).

In the mid-1970s growth in real wages began to level off, unemployment rose as the country experienced a recession (see figures 4.6 and 4.7), and calls for immigration reform began to emerge (Bean, Telles, and Lowell 1987). Frequently, these consisted of restrictionist outcries against the new immigration, often in the form of unsubstantiated claims about the pernicious nature of immigration and its harmful effects on the country. During the 1980s, however, a substantial body of social science research emerged that found little basis for the claims that immigration was generating strongly negative demographic, economic, or social effects. In fact, the research tended to show that immigrants were assimilating socioeconomically within a reasonable period of time, were not exerting very large labor market effects on the wages and unemployment of natives, and were not consuming more in the way of public benefits than they were paying in taxes (Chiswick 1978; Bean, Telles, and Lowell 1987; Borjas and Tienda 1987; Simon 1989; Butcher and Card 1991). To be sure, questions have been raised about whether the skill levels of immigrants have been declining, both within and across countries of origin, because the origin composition of immigration has been changing (Borjas 1990; Lalonde and Topel 1991). But the general conclusion that clearly emerged was that immigration did not appear to be generating much in the way of large effects, whether positive or negative.

Almost all of this research, however, has been based on data collected during the 1970s and early to mid-1980s. The question that remains unanswered is whether similar results would obtain during periods of even greater immigration and continuing slow job and wage growth. Given that these appear to be the conditions characterizing recent years, the issue of the country's capacity to absorb immigration remains a significant question. In the past, this issue has most frequently been addressed in terms of immigration's implications for population growth and, much less frequently, in terms of its implications for economic growth (Easterlin 1982; Morris 1985; Borjas and Tienda 1987).

The volume of immigration relative to population growth is a question that has often been addressed. Many observers have noted that the percentage of foreign-born members in the population, even though rising during the 1970s and 1980s, has remained substantially below the percentage characteristic of

Figure 4.6 Average Hourly Earnings, 1959–1994
(in 1982 dollars)

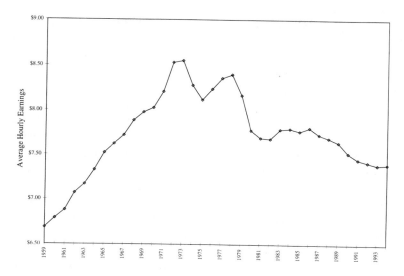

Figure 4.7 Average Unemployment Rate and Civilian
Labor Force

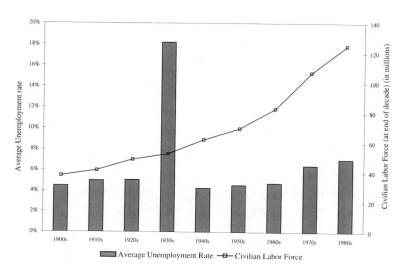

the population in the early part of the twentieth century (Passel 1987; Simon 1987; Borjas 1990; Portes and Rumbaut 1990). In other words, although large in absolute terms relative to the size of the population, immigration during the 1970s and 1980s remained appreciably below the levels occurring in the early twentieth century (see figure 4.1). But interestingly, because of higher fertility and because a larger share of the early-twentieth-century immigrants eventually returned to their countries of origin than appears now to be the case, immigration accounted for roughly similar fractions of population growth in the 1980s as it did at the turn of the century (about 35 percent) (Easterlin 1982; Passel and Edmonston 1994). But whether measured in terms of absolute numbers, in terms of the percentage of foreign-born individuals in the population, or in terms of the contribution of net immigration to population growth, the volume of immigration during the 1980s has not exceeded the immigration to the United States that occurred during the first twenty years of the twentieth century.

Efforts to assess immigration relative to the size of the economy have been much less frequent. Borjas and Tienda (1987) have examined immigration growth relative to the rate of growth in the civilian labor force, noting that "between 1951 and 1980, the U.S. labor force grew by 7.6 million, 12.3 million, and 22.5 million during each successive decade. On the basis of immigrant flows for each of these periods and assuming that all those admitted entered the labor force, recent immigrants could have accounted for at most 33% of this increase in employment during the 1950s, 27% during the 1960s, and 20% during the 1970s." The rate of aggregate unemployment during this period varied from around 4.0 percent in 1950 to around 6.5 percent in 1980 (see figure 4.7). Borjas and Tienda also point out that only about half of all immigrants admitted to the country during this period entered the labor force upon arrival. Thus, however measured, the rate of labor force growth during this period outstripped the rate of growth in immigration.

The economic circumstances of the 1950s, 1960s, and 1970s thus seem to have been more than sufficiently healthy to absorb the numbers of immigrants arriving at the time. During the 1980s, however, several trends reversed. The rate of growth in immigration continued to increase while the rate of growth in the labor force began to decline. From 1970 through 1980, the growth rate in the U.S. labor force dropped to 17 percent from 27 percent during the 1970s. By contrast, the growth rate in the number of new immigrants jumped to 63 percent during the 1980s, compared to 35 percent during the 1970s (see figure 4.1). By 1990 the number of immigrants coming during the decade could have at most accounted for 36 percent of the growth in the labor force, compared to 20 percent during the 1970s (see table 4.6).

Table 4.6 Annual Percentage Change in Civilian Labor Force and the Percentage that Immigrants Make Up of Labor Force Change, by Decade, 1950–1993

Time Period	Annual Percentage Change in Civilian Labor Force	Number of Immigrants as a Percentage of Labor Force Growth
1951–1960	1.8	33.0
1961–1970	1.9	27.0
1971–1980	2.6	20.0
1981–1990	1.6	36.0[1]
1991–1993	1.0	29.0[1]

1. Includes IRCA-adjusted immigrants.

Sources: U.S Bureau of Labor Statistics 1995 and various years; U.S. Immigration and Naturalization Service 1995.

These changes in trends raise the interesting question of how the immigration experience of the late 1980s and early 1990s compares with that experience both during other post-World War II years and in the early part of the twentieth century; that is, how do the volume and growth of immigration compare to growth in the size of the economy? That this question so seldom seems to have been addressed is surprising. To our knowledge, Borjas and Tienda's (1987) examination of growth in immigration relative to growth in the labor force represents one of few attempts to address the issue. Easterlin (1982) has broadly discussed the implications of immigration for growth in GNP, pointing out that, at the simplest level of analysis, aggregate production clearly rises in some direct proportion to increases in immigration but that the challenging problem involves unraveling its effects on per capita output. To the extent that immigrants differ from the general population in characteristics that enhance production (higher proportions working, younger age structures, perhaps greater motivation), the effects would be favorable. To the extent that their characteristics lower production (lower education, less knowledge of English), the effect would be negative. In either case, the effects are not likely to be large because immigrants are still a relatively small fraction of the population and the characteristics of many immigrants are not enormously different from those of natives (Fix and Passel 1994).

The coincidence of trends in economic growth and immigration growth, though not indicative of a causal relationship between the variables, is nonetheless likely to be informative concerning the emergence of conditions likely to influence the reaction of natives to immigration. Figure 4.8 shows average annual rates of growth in per capita GNP for decades of the twentieth century. During the first ten years of this century, when immigration reached the highest levels of any decade in the nation's history (and with respect to a population base less than half its current size), the economy grew faster than did either population or inflation. For example, from 1900 to 1910 the average inflation- and population-adjusted growth rate was 2.8 percent. In other words, the economy expanded 2.8 percent faster than did population after adjusting for inflation. In the 1950s this differential was 1.6 percent, in the 1960s 2.5 percent, in the 1970s 1.8 percent, and in the 1980s 1.6 percent. From 1991 through 1993, it was 0.4 percent. While U.S. economic growth began to increase again in 1992, wage stagnation and decline have continued (see figure 4.6). It is impossible to say whether current economic trends will continue much longer. But because of IRCA's legalization programs and because the Immigration Act of 1990 boosts legal immigration by as much as 40 percent, it is a certainty that high levels of immigration to the United States will continue unless Congress changes the nation's immigration policy. In thinking about the implications of these trends, it is perhaps worth recalling that the last decade with both high levels of immigration and low levels of real per-capita economic growth was 1911–1920. This, of course, was the decade that preceded the outburst of nativism leading to the passage of the National Origins Quota Act in 1924 (Higham 1963).

Figure 4.8 Average Decade Change in Real GNP per Capita

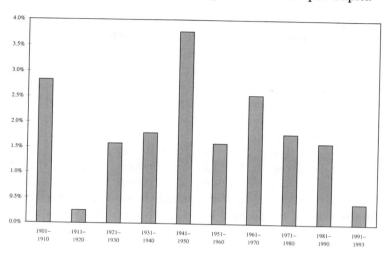

U.S. Immigration Patterns and the Social Contract

Three overarching conclusions emerge from the analyses thus far:
(1) migration flows to the country have been increasing significantly and are beginning to diversify the racial/ethnic composition
of the U.S. population, (2) wage stagnation and uncertainty about
employment security continue as features of the economic context
within which immigrants arrive; and (3) recent substantial
increases in interracial and interethnic marriage not only indicate
the current and future blurring of boundaries between U.S. racial
and ethnic groups (Alba 1990) but also the resilience and growth
of levels of racial and ethnic tolerance in the country. What are the
implications of these major trends for the kinds of factors most
responsible for the recent concerns in the United States about
immigration? In our view, these trends suggest that economic anxieties more than concern over the possibility of increased racial/
ethnic competition and tensions stemming from racially and ethnically diverse immigration flows are at the root of current perceptions that immigration levels to the country are too high.
Otherwise, the dramatic trends toward increased racial and ethnic
intermarriage would be hard to reconcile with expressions of anti-
immigrant sentiment such as Proposition 187 in California.

But if economic anxiety more than growing ethnic prejudice is responsible for rising concerns about immigration, such concerns are no less significant on that account. The combination of the withering of the American Dream and rising immigration levels holds implications for the nature of the social contract in the United States. That contract implies that citizens (and in certain instances other residents) who work hard and obey the nation's laws are eligible for government assistance in the form of health and education benefits and other social services at certain points in their lives, including those times when they are especially economically vulnerable. It is important to emphasize that immigrants do not threaten the social contract per se. That is, they do not jeopardize the social contract just because they are newcomers and not yet citizens. If they succeed economically, do not exert harmful effects on others, and do not receive a disproportionate share of benefits, their entry and the policies regulating (or failing to regulate) their entry are comparatively nonproblematic (Borjas and Tienda 1987). But if they are not successful in their attempts to join the socioeconomic mainstream, create economic problems for others, or disproportionately consume social services and benefits, then immigrants and the policies governing their entry may be seen as potentially threatening the implicit social contract that undergirds the legitimacy of the welfare state.

Even if immigrants are not the direct or indirect cause of negative effects, aggregate economic opportunities may change in ways that may lead to the perception that immigrants are detrimental to the national interest. One of the most important policy-relevant factors in this regard is "the degree to which the labor market can absorb immigrant workers without imposing undue hardships on existing workers" (Morris 1985, 54). An important question is thus the extent to which aggregate conditions that might have made possible the adoption and implementation of certain immigration policies in the past may have changed since those policies were adopted. If such changes have occurred or are perceived to have occurred, they may render less relevant the objectives initially intended by immigration legislation, thus leading to disjunctures in policy objectives and outcomes that may themselves become forces for further policy reform.

The slowdown in the growth rate of the civilian labor force, the stagnation of wages over the past twenty years, the changing spatial and sectoral distribution of jobs by race and ethnicity, and the continuing increase in the growth rate of immigration pose challenges for both analysts and policymakers. Between 1989 and 1992 very little growth occurred in the number of employed people in the United States (as evidenced by a growth rate of less than 0.01 percent). Beginning in early 1993 job growth moved strongly upward until mid-1995, when it ceased. The rise in the numbers of new jobs, however, was accompanied by continued economic restructuring (layoffs) and wage stagnation. Over roughly the same period, total legal immigration continued to increase, boosted by IRCA-related immigration in particular. And starting in 1994 those immigrants who legalized under IRCA (including over 2 million Mexican immigrants) began to become eligible for citizenship, meaning that after they naturalize they can then petition on an unrestricted basis for the additional entry of immediate family members, a phenomenon experts predict will soon boost immigration levels even further.

The recent proposals of the U.S. Commission on Immigration Reform, which was established by the Immigration Act of 1990 and charged with the responsibility of making recommendations for changing all aspects of U.S. immigration policy, provide further testimony that concerns over U.S. immigration levels are rising (Pear 1995). One area of disillusion for some observers derives from doubts about whether legal immigrants should be eligible for affirmative action policies, as they currently are. Lawrence R. Fuchs, for example, notes that "their inclusion in affirmative action programs is a historical accident for which there is no possible justification" (1995, 25–26). As the analyses presented above show, the vast majority of the members of the Hispanic and Asian populations in the United States derives from twentieth-century immigration and immigrants. While a strong case can be made that some members of the U.S. Mexican-origin population in particular experienced historical discrimination, to include recent immigrants under the umbrella of affirmative action policies undermines, in the views of some observers, the legitimacy of both affirmative action and immigration policies (Pear 1995).

It is not unreasonable to think that such situations affect perceptions about the legitimacy of the social contract. It may be the case, however, that these factors are not as significant in affecting perceptions as are economic factors. Supporting this idea is the notion of some analysts that perceptions of the legitimacy of the social contract are especially affected by undocumented immigration (Schuck 1990, 1992). Many observers have argued that an integral part of the country's social contract concerning immigration has consisted of a tacit agreement that good faith efforts to control undocumented immigration are the price paid for the continuation and growth of a moderately expansionist legal immigration policy (Bean and Fix 1992: Fuchs 1990; Schuck 1990, 1992). This contract may have been rendered somewhat more fragile by the apparent failure of IRCA to curb or even slow more than briefly the flow of undocumented migration to the United States (Bean, Edmonston, and Passel 1990; Donato, Durand, and Massey 1992). And the current squeeze on state and local governmental budgets deriving from federal mandates makes it more and more difficult for governments to pay for generous spending policies vis-à-vis immigrants (Fix and Passel 1994).

The challenge to policymakers, then, and one often obscured by the strident and denunciatory claims made by proponents on all sides of the question, is to formulate policies that protect immigrants without embracing the narrowly sectarian rhetoric often espoused by anti-immigration and pro-immigration advocacy groups. The formulation of future U.S. immigration policy confronts obstacles more complex than any it has ever faced. The task is to develop a nuanced immigration policy that gives recognition not only to the realities of difficult domestic labor markets, contradictory affirmative action policies, and financially overburdened state and local governments but also to the emerging fact that the immigration policies of developed countries increasingly involve environmental, developmental, and foreign policy implications as well. Formulating immigration policies that are responsive to the multiple considerations emanating from these various policy domains is a formidable task indeed.

References

Alba, Richard D. 1990. *Ethnic Identity: The Transformation of White America*. New Haven, Conn.: Yale University Press.

Bean, Frank D. 1993. "Immigration Combatants Overlook the New Reality." *Houston Chronicle*, 29 Aug., F1.

Bean, Frank D., Roland Chanove, Robert G. Cushing, Rodolfo de la Garza, Gary Freeman, Charles W. Haynes, and David Spener. 1994. *Illegal Mexican Migration and the United States/Mexico Border: The Effects of Operation Hold-The-Line on El Paso and Juárez*. Washington, D.C.: U.S. Commission on Immigration Reform.

Bean, Frank D., and Michael Fix. 1992. "The Significance of Recent Immigration Policy Reforms in the United States." In *Nations of Immigrants: Australia and the United States in a Changing World*, ed. Gary P. Freeman and James Jupp, 41–55. New York and Sydney: Oxford University Press.

Bean, Frank D., Jeffrey S. Passel, and Barry Edmonston. 1990. *Undocumented Migration to the United States: IRCA and the Experience of the 1980s*. Washington, D.C.: Urban Institute Press.

Bean, Frank D., Eduardo Telles, and Lindsay Lowell. 1987. "Undocumented Migration to the United States: Perceptions and Evidence." *Population and Development Review* 13, no 4: 671–90.

Bean, Frank D., and Marta Tienda. 1987. *The Hispanic Population of the United States*. New York: Russell Sage Foundation.

Bean, Frank D., George Vernez, and Charles B. Keely. 1989. *Opening and Closing the Doors: Evaluating Immigration Reform and Control*. Washington, D.C.: Urban Institute Press.

Berg, Ruth. 1995. "Low Fertility Among Intermarried Mexican-Americans: An Assessment of Three Hypotheses." Ph.D. diss., University of Texas.

Borjas, George. 1990. *Friends and Strangers: The Impact of Immigrants on the U.S. Economy*. New York: Basic.

Borjas, George, and Marta Tienda. 1987. "The Economic Consequences of Immigration." *Science* 235: 645–51.

Bouvier, Leon. 1991. *Peaceful Invasions: Immigration and Changing America*. Washington D.C.: Center for Immigration Studies.

Brimelow, Peter. 1995. *Alien Nation: Common Sense About America's Immigration Disaster*. New York: Random House.

Butcher, Kristin F., and David Card. 1991. "Immigration and Wages: Evidence from the 1980s." *Economic Impact of Immigration* 81, no. 2: 292–96.

Cafferty, Phyllis, Barry R. Chiswick, Andrew Greeley, and Teresa A. Sullivan. 1983. *The Dilemma of American Immigration*. New Brunswick, N.J.: Transaction.

Calavita, Kitty. 1992. *Inside the State: The Bracero Program, Immigration, and the I.N.S.—After the Law*. New York: Routledge.

Campbell, Paul R. 1994. *Population Projections for States, by Age, Sex, Race, and Hispanic Origin: 1993–2020*. P25-1111. Washington, D.C.: U.S. Bureau of the Census.

Chiswick, Barry R. 1978. "The Effect of Americanization on the Earnings of Foreign-born Men." *Journal of Political Economy* 86, no. 5: 897–921.

Donato, Katharine M. 1994. "U.S. Policy and Mexican Migration to the United States, 1942–92." *Social Science Quarterly* 75, no. 4: 705–28.

Donato, Katharine M., Jorge Durand, and Douglas S. Massey. 1992. "Stemming the Tide? Assessing the Deterrent Effects of the Immigration Reform and Control Act." *Demography* 29, no. 2: 3–42.

Easterlin, Richard. 1982. "Economic and Social Characteristics of the Immigrants." *Dimensions of Ethnicity*, ed. S. Thernstrom, 1–35. Cambridge: Harvard University Press, Belknap.

Edmonston, Barry, Sharon M. Lee, and Jeffrey S. Passel. 1994. "Ethnicity, Ancestry, and Exogamy in U.S. Population Projections." Paper presented at the Population Association America meetings, Miami, 5–7 May.

Espenshade, Thomas J. 1995. "Unauthorized Immigration to the United States." *Annual Review of Sociology* 21: 195–216.

Espenshade, Thomas J., and Charles A. Calhoun. 1993. "An Analysis of Public Opinion Toward Undocumented Migration." *Population Research and Policy Review* 12, no. 3: 189–224.

Fix, Michael, and Jeffrey S. Passel. 1994. *Immigration and Immigrants: Setting the Record Straight*. Washington, D.C.: Urban Institute Press.

Fuchs, Lawrence H. 1995. "A Negative Impact of Affirmative Action: Including Immigrants in Such Programs Flies in the Face of Civil Rights." *Washington Post*, national weekly edition, 20–26 Feb., 25–6.

_____. 1990. *The American Kaleidoscope: Race, Ethnicity, and the Civic Culture*. Boston: University Press of New England and Wesleyan University Press.

Goodman, Walter. 1995. "Finding the Real Issue in a Debate About Immigration." *New York Times*, 15 June, Living Arts section, B3.

Hacker, Andrew. 1995. *Two Nations: Black and White, Separate, Hostile, and Unequal*. New York: Ballantine.

Higham, John. 1963. *Strangers in the Land*. New Brunswick, N.J.: Rutgers University Press.

Jasso, Guillermina, and Mark R. Rosensweig, eds. 1990. *The New Chosen People: Immigrants in the United States*. New York: Russell Sage.

Kalmijn, Matthijs. 1993. "Trends in Black/White Intermarriage." *Social Forces* 72, no. 1: 119–146.

LaLonde, R. J., and R. H. Topel. 1991. "Immigrants in the American Labor Market: Quality, Assimilation, and Distributional Effects." *American Economic Review Papers and Proceedings* 91, no. 2: 297–302.

Landau, Ralph. 1988. "U.S. Economic Growth." *Scientific American* 258, no. 6: 44–52.

Levy, Frank. 1987. *Dollars and Dreams: The Changing American Income Distribution*. New York: Russell Sage.

Lieberson, Stanley, and Mary C. Waters. 1988. *From Many Strands: Ethnic and Racial Groups in Contemporary America*. New York: Russell Sage Foundation.

Massey, Douglas S. 1981. "Dimensions of the New Immigration to the United States and the Prospects for Assimilation." *Annual Review of Sociology* 7: 57–85.

McLanahan, Sara, and Lynne Casper. 1995. "Growing Diversity and Inequality in the American Family." In *State of the Union: America in the 1990s*, ed. Reynolds Farley, vol. 2, *Social Trends*, 1–46. New York: Russell Sage Foundation.

Morris, Milton. 1985. *Immigration: The Beleaguered Bureaucracy*. Washington, D.C.: Brookings Institution.

Passel, Jeffrey S. 1987. "Measurement of Ethnic Origin in the Decennial Census." Paper presented at the annual meeting of the American Association for the Advancement of Science, Chicago, 14–18 Feb.

Passel, Jeffrey S., and Barry Edmonston. 1994. "Immigration and Race: Recent Trends in Immigration to the United States." In *Immigration and Ethnicity: The Integration of America's Newest Arrivals*, ed. Barry Edmonston and Jeffrey S. Passel, 31–72. Washington, D.C.: Urban Institute Press.

Pear, Robert. 1995. "Change in Policy for Immigration Is Urged by Panel." *New York Times*, 4 June, 1.

Portes, Alejandro, and Ruben G. Rumbaut. 1990. *Immigrant America: A Portrait*. Berkeley: University of California Press.

Reimers, David M. 1985. *Still the Golden Door*. New York: Columbia University Press.

_____. 1983. "An Unintended Reform: The 1965 Immigration Act and Third World Migration to the United States." *Journal of American Ethnic History* (fall): 9–28.

Schuck, Peter. 1992. "The Politics of Rapid Political Changes: Immigration Policy in the 1980s." *Studies in American Political Development* 6 (spring): 37–82.

_____. 1990. "The Great Immigration Debate." The *American Prospect* (fall): 100–18.

Simon, Julian L. 1989. *The Economic Consequences of Immigration.* Cambridge: Basil Blackwell.

_____. 1987. *Effort, Opportunity and Wealth.* Oxford: Basil Blackwell.

Teitelbaum, Michael S., and Myron Weiner, eds. 1995. *World Migration and U.S. Policy.* New York: Norton.

U.S. Bureau of the Census. 1992. *Census of Population and Housing, 1990. Public Use Microdata Samples U.S.* [Machine-readable datafiles.] Washington, D.C.: Bureau of the Census.

U.S. Bureau of Labor Statistics. 1959–1995. *Monthly Labor Review.* Washington, D.C: U.S. Government Printing Office.

U.S. Commission on Immigration Reform. 1994. *U.S. Immigration Policy: Restoring Credibility.* Washington, D.C.: U.S. Government Printing Office.

U.S. Department of Justice. 1992. *Immigration Reform and Control Act: Report on the Legalized Alien Population.* Washington, D.C.: U.S. Government Printing Office.

U.S. Immigration and Naturalization Service. 1995. *Statistical Yearbook of the U.S. Immigration and Naturalization Service, 1994.* Washington, D.C.: U.S. Government Printing Office.

Warren, Robert. 1992. "Estimates of the Unauthorized Immigrant Population Residing in the United States, by Country of Origin and State of Residence: October 1992." Washington, D.C.: Immigration and Naturalization Service Statistics Division.

_____. 1990. "Annual Estimates of Nonimmigrant Overstays in the United States: 1985–1988." In *Undocumented Migration to the United States: IRCA and the Experience of the 1980s,* Frank D. Bean, Jeffrey S. Passel, and Barry Edmonston, 77–101. Washington, D.C.: The Urban Institute Press.

Warren, Robert, and Jeffrey S. Passel. 1987. "A Count of the Uncountable: Estimates of Undocumented Aliens Counted in the 1980 United States Census." *Demography* 24, no. 3: 375–94.

Waters, Mary C. 1990. *Ethnic Options: Choosing Identities in America.* Berkeley: University of California Press.

Zohlberg, Aristide R. 1992. "Response to Crisis: Refugee Policy in the United States and Canada." In *Immigration, Language, and Ethnicity: Canada and the United States,* d. Barry R. Chiswick, 55–109. Washington, D.C.: AEI Press.

Notes on Contributors

Klaus J. Bade is the chair for modern history and director of the Institute for Migration Research and Intercultural Studies (IMIS) at the University of Osnabrück, FRG. He was a fellow at the Center for European Studies at Harvard University in 1976/77; at St. Antony's College, Oxford, in 1985; and at the Netherlands Institute for Advanced Study (NMIAS), Wassenaar, in 1996/97. He served as chairperson of the German Association for Historical Migration Research (Gesellschaft für Historische Migrationsforschung), editor for the series Studien zur Historischen Migrationsforschung (SHM), and coeditor for the series IMIS-Schriften (Schriften des Instituts für Migrationsforschung und Interkulturelle Studien). He is the author and editor of numerous books on nineteenth- and twentieth-century social and economic history, on the history of colonialism and imperialism as well as on population and migration past and present. His more recent work includes the edited volumes *Deutsche im Ausland—Fremde in Deutschland: Migration in Geschichte und Gegenwart* (Munich 1992), *Das Manifest der 60: Deutschland und die Einwanderung* (Munich 1994), *Menschen über Grenzen—Grenzen über Menschen: Die multikulturelle Herausforderung* (Herne 1995), and *Migration—Ethnizität—Konflikt: Systemfragen und Fallstudien* (Osnabrück 1996) and, as author, *Homo migrans: Wanderungen aus und nach Deutschland—Erfahrungen und Fragen* (Essen 1994) and *Ausländer—Aussiedler—Asyl: Eine Bestandsaufnahme* (Munich 1994).

Frank D. Bean is Ashbel Smith Professor of Sociology and Public Affairs and director of the Population Research Center at the University of Texas at Austin. From 1988 to 1990 he was at the Urban Institute in Washington, D.C., where he served as director of the Program for Research on Immigration Policy and director of the Population Studies Center. A demographer with specializations in Mexican migration to the United States, international migration, family and fertility, the demography of racial and ethnic groups, and population policy, he has published several books, the most recent being *Opening and Closing the Doors: Evaluating Immigration Reform and Control* (with Gerges Vernez and Charles B. Keely), *Mexican and Central American Population and U.S. Immigration Policy* (edited with S. Weintraub and J. Schmandt), *The Hispanic Population of the United States* (with Marta Tienda), *Undocumented Migration to the United States: IRCA and the Experience of the 1980s* (edited with B. Edmonston and J. Passel), *Immigration Categories and the U.S. Job Market* (with Elaine Sorenson), and *Illegal Mexican Migration to the United States and the U.S./Mexico Border* (with several University of Texas colleagues). His current research focuses on various aspects of U.S. immigration patterns and policies and on other demographic issues.

Robert G. Cushing is a professor of sociology and deputy director of the Australian Studies Center at the University of Texas at Austin. From 1972 to 1992 he was professor of sociology at the Australian National University in Canberra, Australia, where he also served as dean of the faculty of letters for six years. His current research focuses on the social and economic consequences of immigration and on various topics in the sociology of development.

Charles Haynes is a doctoral student in the department of sociology at the University of Texas at Austin. His special area of interest and expertise is migration and development, and his doctoral research deals with the internal migration patterns of U.S. immigrants.

Rainer Münz, born in Basel, Switzerland, in 1954, is professor of demography at the Humboldt University, Berlin. Until 1992 he was director of the Institute for Demography of the Austrian Academy of Sciences, Vienna. His main fields of research are European migration, ethnic and linguistic minority issues, and the impact of demographic change on social policy.

Reed Ueda teaches American history at Tufts University. He has been a visiting professor at Brandeis and Harvard. His publications include *Avenues to Adulthood* (1987) and *Postwar Immigrant America* (1994).

Ralf Ulrich, born in Berlin, (East) Germany, in 1954, is assistant professor of demography at the Humboldt University, Berlin. His main fields of research are international migration and the growth of foreign population in Germany, fertility decline and other demographic developments in East Germany, and family planning and population growth in developing countries.

Myron Weiner is Ford International Professor of Political Science at the Massachusetts Institute of Technology and former director of the MIT Center for International Studies. He is the author of and editor of numerous books on India, on political change in developing countries, and on international migration. These include *The Global Migration Crisis: Challenge to States and to Human Rights* (1995), *The New Geopolitics of Central Asia and Its Borderlands* (1995), *Threatened Peoples, Threatened Borders: World Migration and U.S. Policy* (1995), *The Politics of Social Transformation in Afghanistan, Iran, and Pakistan* (1994), *International Migration and Security* (1993), *The Child and the State in India: Child Labor and Education Policy in Comparative Perspective* (1991), *The Indian Paradox* (1989), and *Understanding Political Development* (1986). Professor Weiner has taught at Princeton University, the University of Chicago, and Harvard University and held visiting research appointments at the University of Paris, Hebrew University, Delhi University, and Oxford University. At MIT he chairs the Inter-University Committee on International Migration.

Index

Agency of Lost Words. *See* Reich
   Emigration Agency
Asiatic Barred Zone, 44
Ausseidler. *See under* Germany

Berlin Wall, 22, 67, 73, 74
Bismarck, Otto, 16
Braceros. *See under* Mexico
Brazil, German emigrants to, 15
Burlingame Treaty (1868), 42

Chinese Exclusion Act (1882), 43, 47

Decree against Unacceptable
   Conditions in Emigration
   (1924), 20
Dillingham Immigration
   Commission, 44
Displaced Persons Act (1948), 125

Emigration clubs, 13
Engels, Friedrich, 13

Fabri, Friedrich, 14
Family reunion, 48, 67, 72, 82,
   91–92, 103, 123, 139
Federal Administration Office,
   20–21
Federal Emigration Agency, 20
Federal Emigration Office, 20
Forced repatriation, 110n 2, 111n 8

Geneva Convention Relating to
   Status of Refugees, 88, 89
Gentleman's Agreement, 43
German-American clubs, 57
German Colonial Empire, 15
German Colonial Society, 16
German colonialism, 14–15
German emigrants to United
   States, vii–ix, 4–9, 54–55, 55–59
German Foreigners Register, 92
German-Italian Treaty (1955), 23
German-language newspapers in
   U.S., 57–58
German Mennonites, 42
German Reich, 15, 16
"Germannness" (*Deutschtum*), 14,
   19, 21
Germany.
   as de facto immigration country,
      1, 23–24, 28–29, 30, 65, 110
   as emigration country, xi–xii, 18
   asylum seekers in, xvi, 25,
      84–90, 97, 103
   Ausseidler in, x–xi, xii, 4, 21, 25,
      66, 67, 69, 70–71, 75, 76, 103,
      107
   citizenship of, xii
   emigration from, 4, 13, 14,
      75–77
   emigration law (1849), 13
   ethnic Germans. *See* Ausseidler